English in Perspective

Student's Book 1

Dalzell + Edgar

Oxford University Press
1988

Contents chart

Unit number	Main language point	Other language points	Topic area	Notions/Functions
1	*Have got*	Contractions What? Colours Possession Word order	Personal possessions Personal details: families, jobs	Identifying Describing
2	Prepositions of place	Spelling: singular/plural nouns Articles	Everyday objects in strange places Household objects	Asking and saying where things are
3	Imperatives	Possession	Domestic tasks Household objects and rooms	Understanding and giving instructions
4	Simple Present tense	Question words	Study habits Machines	Personal habit and routine Describing how things work Asking for information
5	*Will:* future Simple Present tense	Word order with Simple Present	Weather Dates/months/seasons	Describing a process Predicting
6	*Can*	Adverbs Possession	Language analysis Messages and signs	Ability Polite requests Possibility Understanding messages
7	*Let's* *Could*	*Will* – intention Prepositions of time	Emergency situations Performance art Airports	Making suggestions Stating intentions Understanding instructions
8	Comparatives and superlatives of adjectives		Cars Travel	Making comparisons Stating opinions Agreeing and disagreeing
9	Countable and uncountable nouns – *much, many, some, any*	*Too/enough*	Language analysis Food – quantities and containers	Expressing quantity
10	'O' Conditional	*Must* Contractions	Facts Superstitions Language learning Office layout	Talking about beliefs and opinions
11	Present Continuous tense	Spelling – Present Participle	Actions Social change Railway stations	Describing actions – commentary Talking about social change Stating intention Understanding instructions

Unit number	Main language point	Other language points	Topic area	Notions/Functions
12	*Was/Were*	Past time adverbials *What...like?*	Travel World events	Asking and answering questions about past events Understanding contexts and situations Revision
13	Simple Past tense	*Some/any/every* compounds	Language analysis Mystery stories	Narrating past events Asking about the past
14	Simple Past tense	Spelling	Bank robberies	Narrating past events
15	Linkers – *a moment later, then, suddenly, and*	Verb + *like*	Sound stories	Narrating past events
16	Past Continuous tense		Jewel theft Car accident	Narrating/describing past events
17	*Like* + noun *Like* + verb + *-ing*	Idioms Likes/dislikes	Rats Personal preferences	Expressing likes/ dislikes/feelings
18	Adverbs of frequency Word order		Gestures Social situations Personal characteristics/style	Routine and habit Expressing anger/ being rude Describing people
19	*To need* *To have to*	Clauses of purpose – *to*	Expeditions Bureaucracy	Necessity Obligation Making plans
20	*Going to*	Future time adverbials	Political plans Families	Stating intention Predicting
21	1st Conditional	*How* questions Simple Present in the future	Holidays and travel information Directions	Making plans Suggesting and comparing alternatives Understanding directions
22	*Will have to* *Going to have to* *Have (got) to*		Towns and town amenities Future trends and developments	Future obligations Predicting Speculating about the future
23	Revision of future forms	Preposition + *-ing*	Business meeting	Making plans Making suggestions
24	Revision of past forms		Telling stories	Narrating past events

Exercise Key   *page 137*

Grammar Review   *page 143*

Unit 1

1 Listen to the tape.

Identify:
the watch
the bag
the shirt

HOT SUMMER BUYS, STYLISH AND CHEAP

THE CHEAP

Cheap, fun watches in lots of exciting colours. Steel or plastic. From £3.50 to £12

THE PRACTICAL

Stylish, practical bags with lots of space. From £7.50 to £25

THE CHEERFUL

Bright, cheerful shirts for hot sunny days. Cool cotton. From £4.00 to £11.50

2 Pairs

Partner A:
Choose a watch.
Describe it to your partner.
Now choose a bag and a shirt.
Describe them to your partner.
Partner B:
Find the thing your partner describes.

Useful Language

it's sort of yellow
it's got two pockets
it's got a zip
it's got a red strap

Has it got a . . . ?
Yes, it has/No, it hasn't.

3 Families

This is the Barker family.
Below is the family tree.

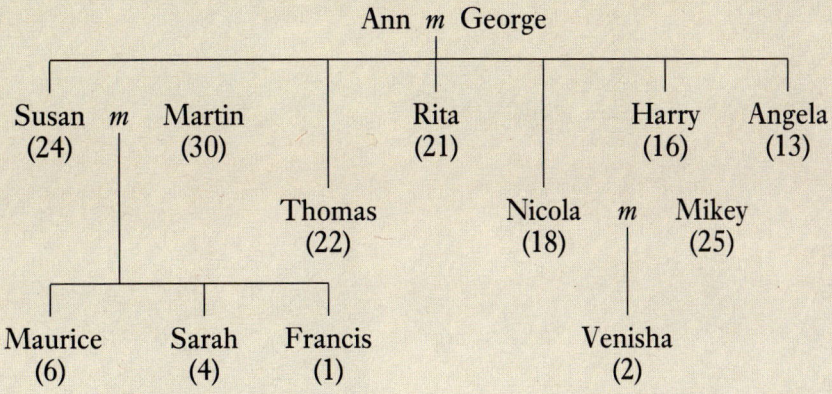

Read this and look at the tree.

Ann's husband is George. They have got six children, three daughters and three sons. Two of their children are married. Susan is married to Martin and they have three children. Nicola and her husband, Mikey, have got one daughter. So Ann has got four grandchildren: two grandsons and two granddaughters.

Now read this and complete.

Francis is the baby of the family. He has one _____, Maurice, and one _____, Sarah. His _____ are Susan and Martin. His _____ is George. George's wife Ann is Francis's _____.

What's your father's name?
And your mother's?

Draw your family tree for three generations. Label the relationships.

1

4 Jobs

Match the pictures with these jobs.

mechanic
computer operator
administrator
bank clerk
cashier
health worker
engineer
factory worker
cabin attendant
receptionist
musician
sailor
teacher
builder
farmer

Have you got a job?

Yes. – Is there a picture of your job here?
    What is your job?
No. – Choose a picture.
    What is the job in your picture?

What's your partner's job?
Find out about other people.

Language   1

have got   **Form**

Affirmative: Subject + has/have + got   (She's got) / (I've got)   *She's got a new car.*

Negative: Subject + has/have + not + got   (hasn't) / (haven't)   *I haven't got a job.*

Interrogative: has/have + subject + got   *Have you got a job?* / *What have you got?*

Use

1 Possession *I've got a yellow watch.*
2 Physical characteristics *He's got black hair.*
3 Relationships (family and friends) *They've got four children.*

Contractions   It's = a contraction.
's = is or has?

a It's pink and white. = _____
b It's got three pockets. = _____
c It's got green eyes. = _____
d It's very old. = _____

What   Match the question and the answer.

1 What's your job?   a It's a pink elephant.
2 What's this?   b It's sort of blue.
3 What time is it?   c I'm a factory worker.
4 What colour is your new car?   d John.
5 What's your name?   e It's half past six.

Colours   Yellows

yellow   bright yellow   dark yellow   light yellow   sort of yellow

Look at these.   a   b   c   d   e

Which one is:
bright red?
red?
sort of red?
                        a   b   c   d   e

Which ones are:
dark blue?
light blue?

Name the colours in the classroom.

1

Possessive 's'

Look around you. Who can you see?

Make sentences like this:
Filippo's hair is long.
Gertrude's trousers are green.

Possessive adjectives

Match the sentences to the pictures.

1 It's **my** pen.
2 It's **his** watch.
3 It's **your** stereo.
4 It's **our** case.
5 They're **her** books.
6 It's **their** car.
7 They're **your** glasses.

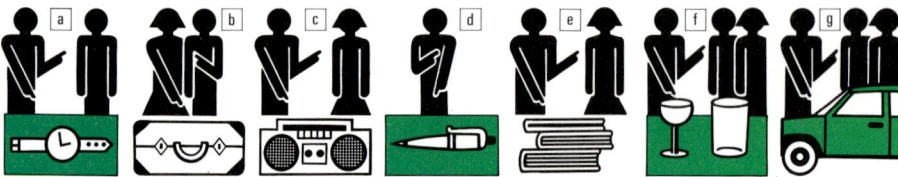

Word order

The order of words is important in English.
Look at these phrases:

the yellow sun
a blue bag
an old man
a small child

There are three words in each phrase.
Which word is the noun, the article, the adjective?

Can we say:
blue typewriter a;
man a cheerful;
the moon silver;
a cheap watch;
practical a person?

What is the correct order/rule?

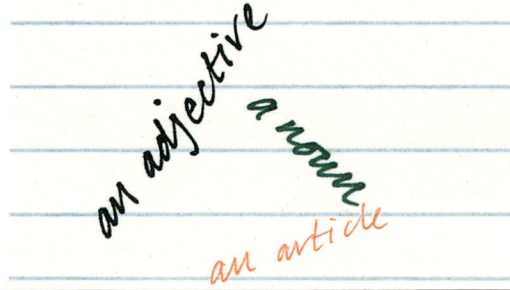

Vocabulary

Check you understand these words. They are all verbs. Use a dictionary. Find one example of each in Unit 1.

to listen, to identify, to choose, to describe, to find, to read, to complete, to draw, to match, to look, to make, to write

Practice in Listening

Listen and match the speakers to the pictures.

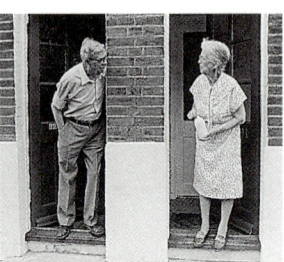

Unit 2

1

What's the man got in his left hand?
What's he got in his right hand?
What's on the top shelf?
What's under the chair?
What's above the man?

Where's the man?
Where's the typewriter?
Where's the spoon?
Where's the chair?
Where's the briefcase?

2

2 Listen.

Draw these things on the picture.
Or draw an arrow from each object to its place on the picture.

3 Pairs

Draw the Beach Scene. Think of six everyday objects. Put them in your picture. Describe your drawing to your partner.
Draw your partner's picture.

4 Pairs

Partner A: Look at the picture of the kitchen on page 134. Partner B: Look at the picture of the kitchen on page 136.

Eight things are in different places in the two pictures. Ask your partner questions to find out what things they are. Write down the exact places of the eight things in your picture. Compare your information with your partner's.

Useful Language

Where's the ...
It's under/on top of/in the ....
There's a ... next to/in/on the ....
Is the ... next to/in/on the ....
Yes, it is. No, it isn't.
I don't know.

Language 2

Prepositions

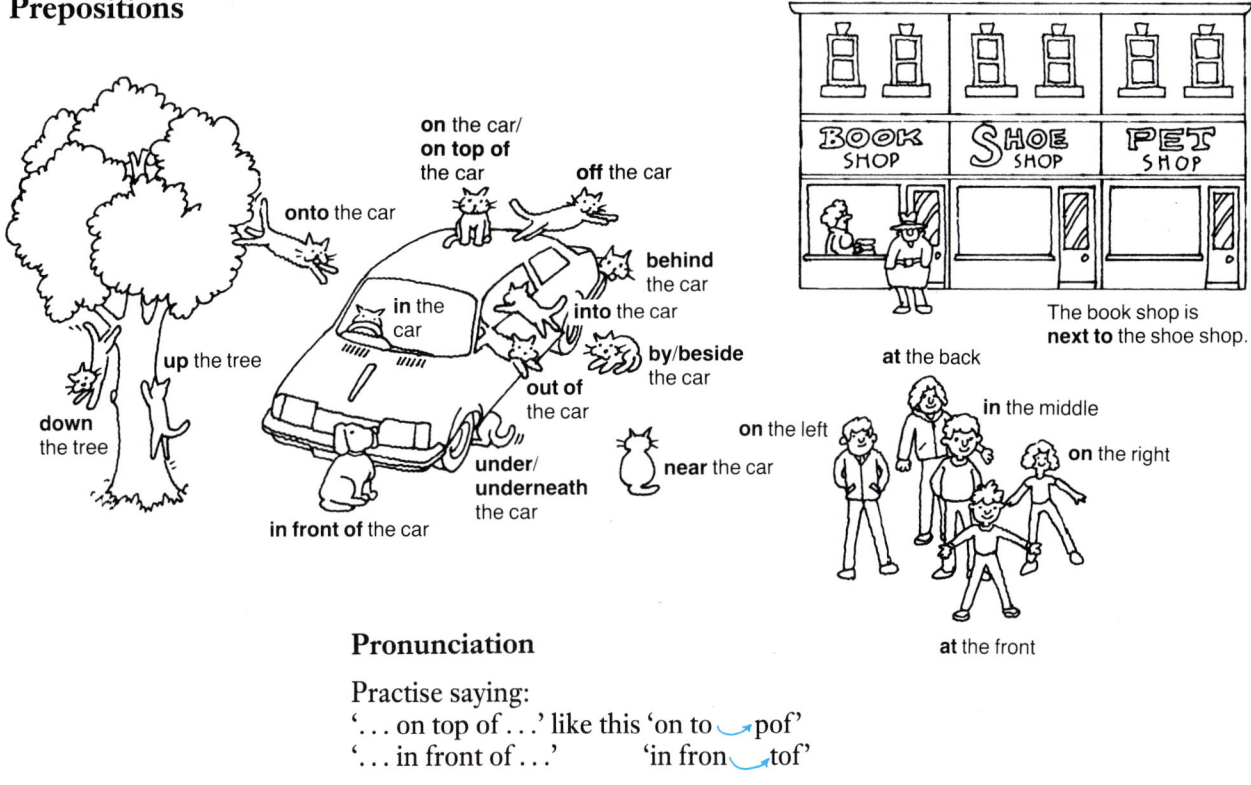

Pronunciation

Practise saying:
'... on top of ...' like this 'on to pof'
'... in front of ...' 'in fron tof'

Spelling: singular and plural nouns

Regular

1 cat/s, book/s, car/s, student/s, tree/s, table/s, teacher/s.
   Rule: Noun + s.
2 bus/es, church/es, box/es, bush/es.
   Rule: 's', 'ch', 'x', 'sh' nouns + es.
3 baby/babies, spy/spies, study/studies.
   Rule: Nouns that end in 'consonant + y' → 'consonant + ies'.
4 day/days, way/ways, guy/guys, key/keys.
   Rule: Nouns that end in 'vowel + y' → 'vowel + y + s'.

Irregular

Here are some: man/men, foot/feet, knife/knives.
Find out the plural for: child, woman, tooth.

Pronunciation: Plural nouns

'-s' is pronounced [s] after voiceless sounds, [z] after voiced sounds.
'-s' and '-es' are pronounced [-ɪz] after the sounds [s], [z], [ʃ], [ʒ], [tʃ] and [dʒ].

Practise saying:
cats[s], cars[z], buses[ɪz]
students[s], spies[z], boxes[ɪz]

2

Articles: a/an/the

[A]

Find a dog with a black tail.
Find the dog with black ears.
Find the dog with a collar.
Find a dog with a spot.

Name a world leader.
Name the leader of your country.
Name a city in your country.
Name the capital city of your country.

[B]

There is a man and a dog in a park. The dog has got a ball and the man has got a bag. There is a tree in the park.

new information → *a*   old information → *the*

Fill in *a* or *the*:
There is _____ man and _____ woman in _____ café. _____ man has _____ cup of coffee. _____ woman has _____ glass of milk. Behind _____ woman there is _____ picture.

2

Pronunciation: a/an

Say these words:
bed, apple, elephant, sofa, university, hour, door, unit, orange, horse, ice-cream, uncle, union, kitchen, island.

Make two lists:
1 the first sound of the word is a vowel sound;
2 the first sound of the word is a consonant sound.

Practise saying:
the words in list 1 with *an*, e.g. a napple;
the words in list 2 with *a*, e.g. /ə/ bed.

Vocabulary

Look at the picture of the kitchen on page 134. Make a list of all the objects. Use a dictionary.

sink, cupboard, ...

Practice in Listening

Look at these pictures.
Listen. Match the speakers to the pictures.

Unit 3

1
  a Look quickly at these texts. They are all instructions. Match each text to the picture.
  b Look again at text (a) (correcting fluid). The verbs are:
affirmative – *shake, close, keep*
negative – *do not drink, (do not) inhale.*

These are examples of the Imperative (see page 16). We use the Imperative for instructions.
Choose one of the texts. List the verbs and find out their meaning.

a Shake well. Close cap tightly after use. Do not drink or inhale. Keep out of children's reach.

b CALPOL 280ml
TAKE ONE 5ml SPOONFUL
FOUR TIMES A DAY
AT NIGHT
WHEN REQUIRED
SHAKE WELL BEFORE USE
27/04/84
KEEP OUT OF CHILDREN'S REACH

c Drop the beans in 1½ pints of cold water. Add 1 level teaspoon of salt, bring to the boil and simmer for 12 mins.

d Remove battery cover. Insert four R14 batteries. Align + and – polarities. Replace cover.

e First wet your face and throat. Squeeze about a teaspoonful into the palm of your hand. Add warm water and vigorously work into a creamy lather. Apply to your face and throat keeping away from your eyes. Massage gently with your fingertips. Rinse well and pat dry.

f DIRECTIONS: Place the filter bag in a cup, or in a warmed pot. (One per person.) Add boiling water. Leave for 2-4 minutes to bring out the full flavour. Add a slice of lemon or a spoonful of honey to taste.

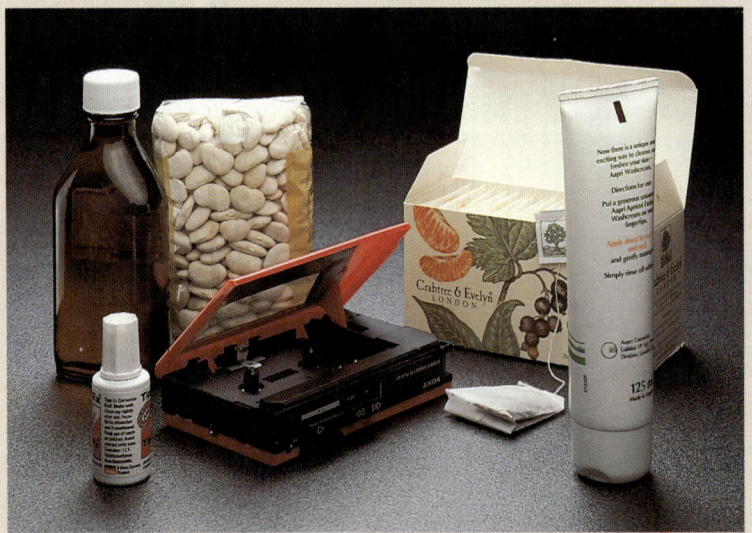

2 Look at this list:
Start a car	Use a video	Use a car wash	Prepare a baby's bottle
Use a dishwasher	Prepare dinner	Put up a tent	Make a fire

Listen. Which instructions are on the tape?

3 Read this instruction leaflet.

Underline the examples of the Imperative (affirmative and negative).
Write the text for number 3.

Première Radiant Heater Safety Instructions

TO BE KEPT WITH THE HEATER

1 ALWAYS use Heater in accordance with instructions supplied with each Heater. Keep instructions in a safe place.

2 DO NOT place clothes or other materials on the Heater, as apart from the danger of fire their presence could affect the efficient working of the appliance.

3

4 DO NOT move Heater from room to room when it is lit.

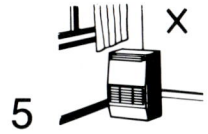

5 DO NOT position Heater alongside a wall or near curtains, etc. ALWAYS face Heater towards centre of room.

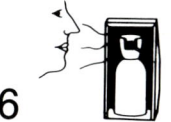

6 A leak will smell

VENTILATION Adequate ventilation must be provided in rooms in which the Heater is installed.
DO NOT CHANGE CYLINDER IN THE PRESENCE OF NAKED LIGHTS

---

4 Pairs

One of you take picture 1. The other take picture 2.

[A] Each of you look at your picture for two or three minutes. Think. Don't speak. Use the pictures to organize some instructions in your mind. Don't write. When you are ready, give your instructions to your partner.

[B] Each of you think of a simple task that you can do, e.g. prepare a snack or make a hot drink. Draw a set of pictures. Use a dictionary to find any words you need. Give your partner a set of instructions.

Language

Imperative

Form

The infinitive of verbs is: *to* + verb
The imperative form is: ~~to~~ + verb

to shake – infinitive
shake – imperative

The Imperative does not change for singular or plural.
Affirmative: *Come here, Paul. Come here, boys.*
Negative: *Do not* or *Don't* – *Don't move the heater.*

Use

1 To give orders *Be quiet!*
2 To give warnings *Be careful!*
3 To instruct *Press the green button.*

Possession

1 The possessive '*s*' is used for people and animals:
   Marie's car.   *The dog's plate.*

Rule: The possessive of singular nouns = Noun + apostrophe + s[z].

2 Look at these:
   1 teacher + 1 coat = the teacher's coat
   1 teacher + 3 coats = the teacher's coats
   3 teachers + 3 coats = the teachers' coats
   3 teachers + 1 coat! = the teachers' coat

Rule: The possessive of regular plurals = Noun + ___ + ___

3 Look at these:
   the dog's bone   the child's toys   the cats' basket
   the man's kitchen   the babies' bottles   the girls' jobs
   the women's office   the children's garden

Look at the middle words – the first nouns. Which are singular, which are plural? Which are the irregular plurals?

Rule: The possessive of irregular plurals = Noun + ___ + ___

Vocabulary

Check you understand these verbs. Use a dictionary.
Find one example of each in Unit 3.

to start, to use, to prepare, to shake, to dry, to add, to light, to apply, to drop

Practice in Listening

Look at these pictures.
Listen. Match the pictures to the people speaking.

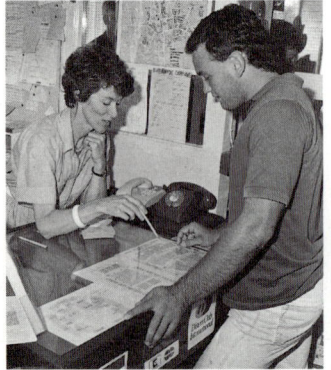

Developments 3

[A] Complete the instructions.

1 Put card/coin into slot.
2 _____ into position.
3 _____ off the engine.
4 _____ the button.
5 ___ ___ ___
6 Wait until the programme is finished.

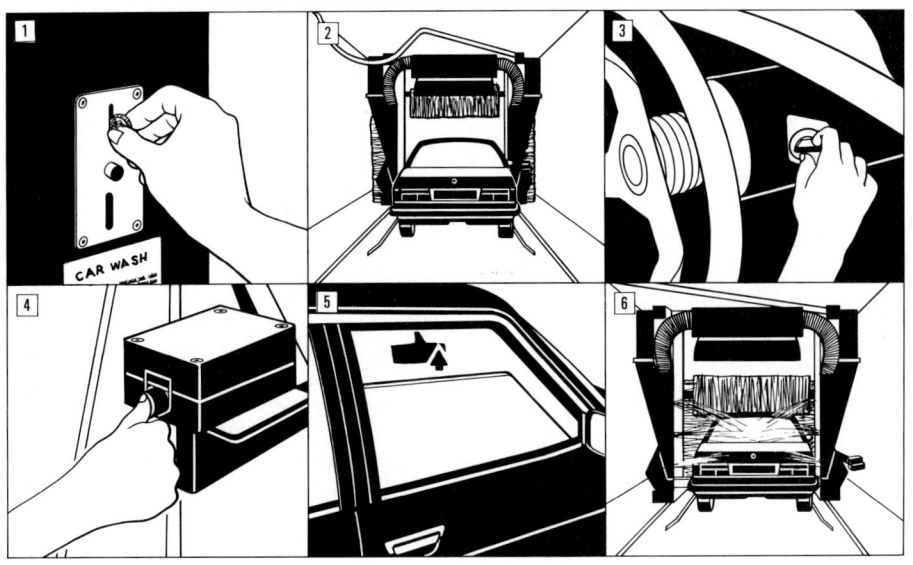

[B] Match the warnings and orders to the pictures.

a Mind your head!
b Get lost!
c Look out!
d Don't move!
e Be quiet!

3

[C] Rooms

1

Name the things in the room.
Write the words.

2 Look at this list of things:

saucepan, bed, cup, alarm clock, nailbrush, knife, toothbrush, pyjamas, pillow, towel, spoon, razor

Where do you find these things?
Write the name of the room in the middle bubble. Fill in the words.

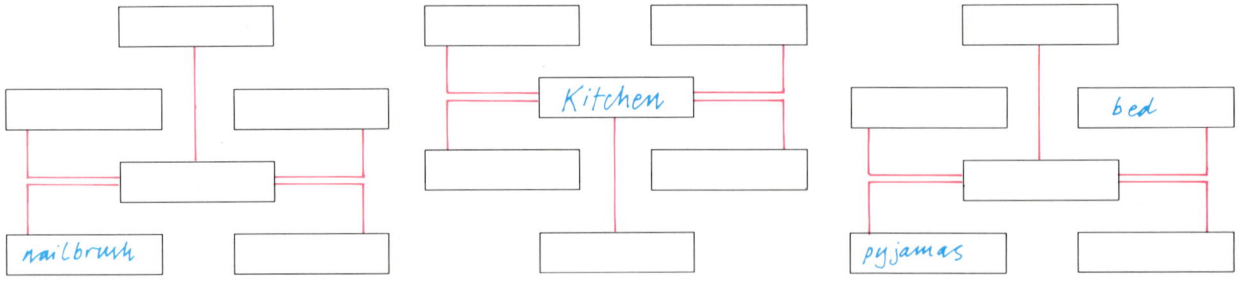

Think of other things for these rooms. Add more bubbles.

Pronunciation

We say – na<u>il</u>brush   <u>ki</u>tchen   py<u>ja</u>mas
We stress the part of the word that is underlined.

Underline the stress in:
saucepan   alarm   pillow   razor   bathroom   bedroom

Underline the stress in the words you wrote in C2 above. Use a dictionary to check.

Unit 4

1 Where do you study . . . ?

When do you study . . . ?

2

Grammar Destroys Marriage

The Morris family have a problem. Daniel, an unemployed salesman and father of four, studies eight hours a day in the bathroom. Every morning at 4.00 a.m. he goes into the bathroom, locks the door and turns on his stereo. Loud music blasts out until 12.00 midday. What does he do in there? He studies French grammar! This is his four- teenth attempt to learn a language and this time, says Daniel, 'I'll do it!' His wife Anne Marie doesn't share his optimism. She says she wants a divorce.

19

3 Look at the questionnaire on study habits.
Complete the information for Daniel Morris.
Find out about other people. Ask questions.

STUDY HABITS

	Mr Morris		
Study Where			
When			
How often			

Study with music			
with the TV			
in silence			

Study and eat	Sometimes		
and smoke	No		
and drink	Sometimes – Tea and coffee		

What else...?	I sit in the bath		

Language 4

Simple present tense   **Form**

Affirmative: Subject + | verb | *They live in Ontario.*
                          | verb + s | *She lives in Ontario.*

Negative: Subject + | do | + not (don't) + verb | *We don't live in Paris.*
                      | does | (doesn't) | *He doesn't live in Paris.*

Interrogative: | do | + subject + verb | *Do you live in Australia?*
                 | does | | *Does she live in Australia?*
                                          | *Where do you live?*
                                          | *Where does she live?*

Use

1 Habit; things that happen again and again *He studies in the bathroom every day.*
2 Facts *I live in Australia.*
3 Feelings *I like coffee.*
4 Thoughts *I think it's good.*

Question words

[A] These are common question words:
what, where, when, why, who, how, which

What asks about 'things'. Match the other question words to these:
reason, time, choice, way/manner, place, person, things

[B] *Why/because*

Why do you study? | Because I like it.
                  | Because I want a good job.
                  | Because I have got exams.

Why do **you** study?
Why does your partner study?

[C] *Who*

Maggie telephones Ronnie every Sunday.

a Who telephones Ronnie? _____
b Who does Maggie telephone? _____

Diana drives Charles to work every day.

Write the questions:
c _____? Diana
d _____? Charles

4

[D] *How*

Choose the correct answer to these *how* questions.
1 How do you get to the centre of town?
2 How do you cut cheese?
3 How do you make that?
4 How does that machine work?

a With a knife.
b The engine turns the wheels.
c By bus.
d With cheese and white sauce.

Now look at these:
How fast does he type? ▷ Very slowly.
How old are the childen? ▷ Ten, six, and three months.
How tall is she? ▷ About one and a half metres.

Rule: How + _____ + verb phrase asks for a description.

[E] *How often*

How often do you go to the library? Which of these are possible answers?

once or twice a week
never
on Monday
every week
in the evening
just sometimes
at 8 o'clock

Vocabulary

Look through this unit (page 19 – page 23) and list ten words you want to learn. Choose the words which interest you; the ones which are useful to you. Check the meaning in the dictionary. Write one sentence with each word.

Practice in Listening

Look at these pictures.
Listen. Match the conversations to the pictures.

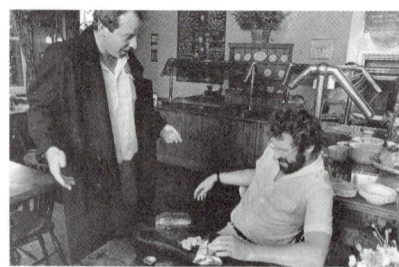

Developments 4

[A] Study the picture. Look at the description and fill in the blanks. Use these verbs. Put the verbs in the correct form.

to fall, to light, to take, to drive, to heat, to open, to eat, to tell, to put

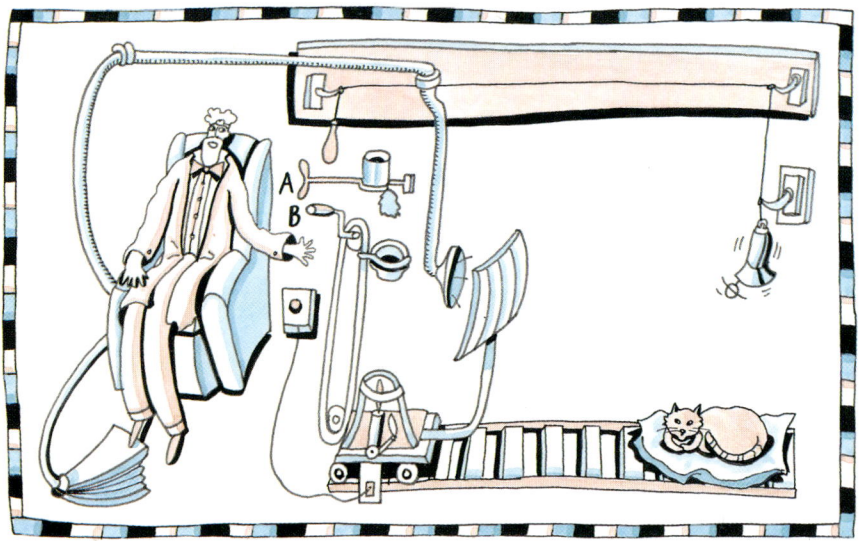

Handle A _____ the tin of cat food and the food _____ onto the plate.
Handle B _____ the plate on the train.
The button _____ the candle and the candle _____ the food.
The pump _____ the train and the train _____ the food to the cat.
The bell _____ the cat 'It's dinner time'.
The cat _____ the food.

[B] Design a machine to feed your pet fish. Use these pictures. Add other pieces if you want.

How does your machine work? Write some notes.

23

Unit 5

1 Where do you see these? What information do they give?

Cool with showers
Guardian 6.3.84.

Outlook: rain
Sunday Times 29.7.84.

Drizzle will spread
Guardian 22.6.86.

Sunny periods
Guardian 7.8.84.

Clouding over
Sunday Times 24.6.84.

Sun and showers
Guardian 13.7.84.

The weather
MAINLY dry and mild. Details, back page.
Guardian 6.3.84.

The weather
Dry with sunny periods, but a cloudy start in some eastern districts. Mostly very warm. (Details, page 2.)
Observer 22.7.84.

Mostly dry and sunny
Sunday Times 5.8.84.

2 Relief Rain

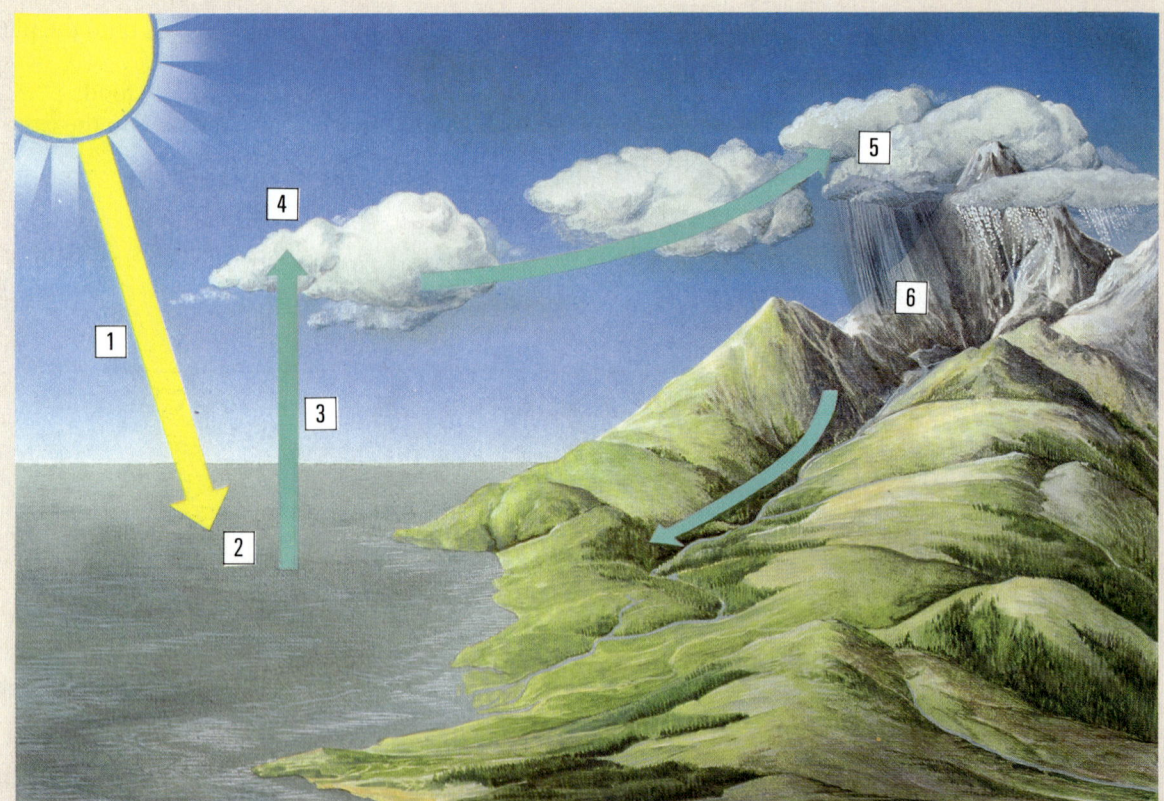

1 The sun heats the air above the sea.
2 The water evaporates in the warm air.
3 This warm, wet air rises and cools.
4 Now cool and wet, the air condenses and forms clouds.
5 When these clouds meet high land, they rise.
6 As they rise, rain falls. It runs into rivers and goes back to the sea.

3 Convection Rain

Find the Tropics on your world map.

Convection rainfall occurs in some areas of the Tropics. The tropical sun is very strong and heats the land to very high temperatures. The sun and the hot land together heat the air, which rises. As the hot air rises, cold air moves in and pushes the hot air up extremely high. There the air cools, the water in the air condenses and enormous clouds form. In the early afternoon very heavy rain falls.

Look at the diagram.
What happens at each point?
1 *The sun heats the land.*
2 _____
3 _____
4 _____
5 _____
6 _____
7 _____

4 Weather

[A] Draw the correct symbol beside each word.

word	symbol
sun	
heavy rain	
strong wind	
clouds	
sunny periods	
showers	
storms	
snow	

[B] Pair these words:

showery
to cool
cold
to fall
sunshine
to heat
wet
dry
hot
rain
sunny periods
to rise

Which words are verbs, adjectives and nouns?

5

5 Listen.

These weather forecasts are for four different English speaking countries: Britain, Jamaica, Australia and Canada. Find the countries on your world map.

Write the name of the country beside the weather forecast:
Hot with storms _____
Variable – sunny periods and showers _____
Sunny with snow showers _____
Hot and dry _____

Listen to the pronunciation of *'ll*. Write down the words. Practise saying *it'll be, there'll be*.

6 Groups/Pairs

What is the weather forecast today?
Predict: What will the weather be tomorrow?

Other predictions:
What is the next big sports event in the world?
Who will win?

Useful Language

It'll be hot/cold/showery.
They say there'll be showers/storms.
I think it'll be hot and sunny.

Who do you think'll win the match/the race?
We'll win.
No, they won't.   Yes, they will.

This is a traditional children's rhyme.

Rain, rain go away. Come again another day. Rain, rain go to Spain, Don't you dare come back again.

Language 5

will

Form

We use *will* for all persons.
Affirmative: Subject + will ('ll) + verb *It'll rain.*
Negative: Subject + will not (won't) *It won't rain.*
Interrogative: Will + subject + verb *Will it rain?*

Use

To make a prediction about the future

Note: There are many other ways of talking about the future in English. See Units 11, 21 and 22.

Word order

1 *She* = subject
   drives = verb
   a Volkswagen = object

Look at these sentences. Many are incorrect. Fill in the brackets.

a A Volkswagen she drives
   (object) (_____) (_____)
b Drives she a Volkswagen
   (verb) (_____) (_____)
c She drives a Volkswagen
   (subject) (_____) (_____)
d Drives a Volkswagen
   (_____) (_____)

Which is the correct sentence?
Rule: The word order in a statement is _____

2 *Do* = auxiliary
   you = subject
   like = verb
   rain = object

Look at these interrogative sentences. Fill in the brackets.

a You do rain like?
   (_____) (_____) (_____) (_____)
b Do you like rain?
   (_____) (_____) (_____) (_____)
c Like you rain?
   (_____) (_____) (_____)
d Rain like you?
   (_____) (_____) (_____)

Which is the correct sentence?
Rule: The word order in an interrogative sentence is _____

3 Look at these negative sentences.

a I don't watch TV
   (_____) (_____) (_____) (_____)
b I do TV not watch
   (_____) (_____) (_____) (_____)
c TV watch do not I
   (_____) (_____) (_____) (_____)

Which is the correct sentence?
Rule: The word order in a negative sentence is _____

5

Vocabulary

Some words look the same in different languages:
to use (English) *usare* (Italian) *user* (French).

Look through this unit and make a list of all the words which look similar to words in your language. Check the meaning carefully. Is it the same? Write sentences for the English words.

Practice in Listening

Read the questions below. Then listen to the tape and answer the questions.

a Are they children/teenagers/young adults/
middle-aged people/old people?
b Do they know each other/not know each other?
c Do they like each other? Do they dislike each other?
d Are they unfriendly/friendly?

Developments 5

[A] Dates

We say: 'the first of January nineteen eighty-six'
We write: 1st January 1986

So *22nd March 1975* is: 'the twenty-second of March nineteen seventy-five'

Practise saying:

3rd April 1922   22nd July 1131
10th November 1815   15th October 2044
18th June 1998   19th January 1919
31st May 2000   6th August 1701

[B] Months

Many British people remember the number of days in each month only with the help of a rhyme. Use this information to complete the rhyme below.

	JANUARY	FEBRUARY	MARCH	APRIL	MAY	JUNE
M	4 11 18 25	1 8 15 22 29	7 14 21 28	4 11 18 25	2 9 16 23 30	6 13 20 27
T	5 12 19 26	2 9 16 23	1 8 15 22 29	5 12 19 26	3 10 17 24 31	7 14 21 28
W	6 13 20 27	3 10 17 24	2 9 16 23 30	6 13 20 27	4 11 18 25	1 8 15 22 29
T	7 14 21 28	4 11 18 25	3 10 17 24 31	7 14 21 28	5 12 19 26	2 9 16 23 30
F	1 8 15 22 29	5 12 19 26	4 11 18 25	1 8 15 22 29	6 13 20 27	3 10 17 24
S	2 9 16 23 30	6 13 20 27	5 12 19 26	2 9 16 23 30	7 14 21 28	4 11 18 25
S	3 10 17 24 31	7 14 21 28	6 13 20 27	3 10 17 24	1 8 15 22 29	5 12 19 26
	JULY	AUGUST	SEPTEMBER	OCTOBER	NOVEMBER	DECEMBER
M	4 11 18 25	1 8 15 22 29	5 12 19 26	3 10 17 24 31	7 14 21 28	5 12 19 26
T	5 12 19 26	2 9 16 23 30	6 13 20 27	4 11 18 25	1 8 15 22 29	6 13 20 27
W	6 13 20 27	3 10 17 24 31	7 14 21 28	5 12 19 26	2 9 16 23 30	7 14 21 28
T	7 14 21 28	4 11 18 25	1 8 15 22 29	6 13 20 27	3 10 17 24	1 8 15 22 29
F	1 8 15 22 29	5 12 19 26	2 9 16 23 30	7 14 21 28	4 11 18 25	2 9 16 23 30
S	2 9 16 23 30	6 13 20 27	3 10 17 24	1 8 15 22 29	5 12 19 26	3 10 17 24 31
S	3 10 17 24 31	7 14 21 28	4 11 18 25	2 9 16 23 30	6 13 20 27	4 11 18 25

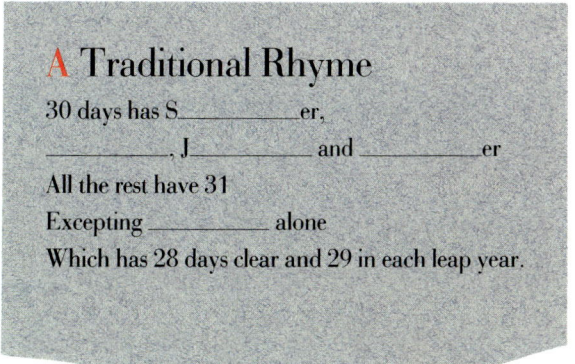

A Traditional Rhyme

30 days has S_____er,
_____, J_____ and _____er
All the rest have 31
Excepting _____ alone
Which has 28 days clear and 29 in each leap year.

How often do we get a leap year? Give an example.

5

[C] Seasons

Many places in the world have different seasons. Read the short texts below.

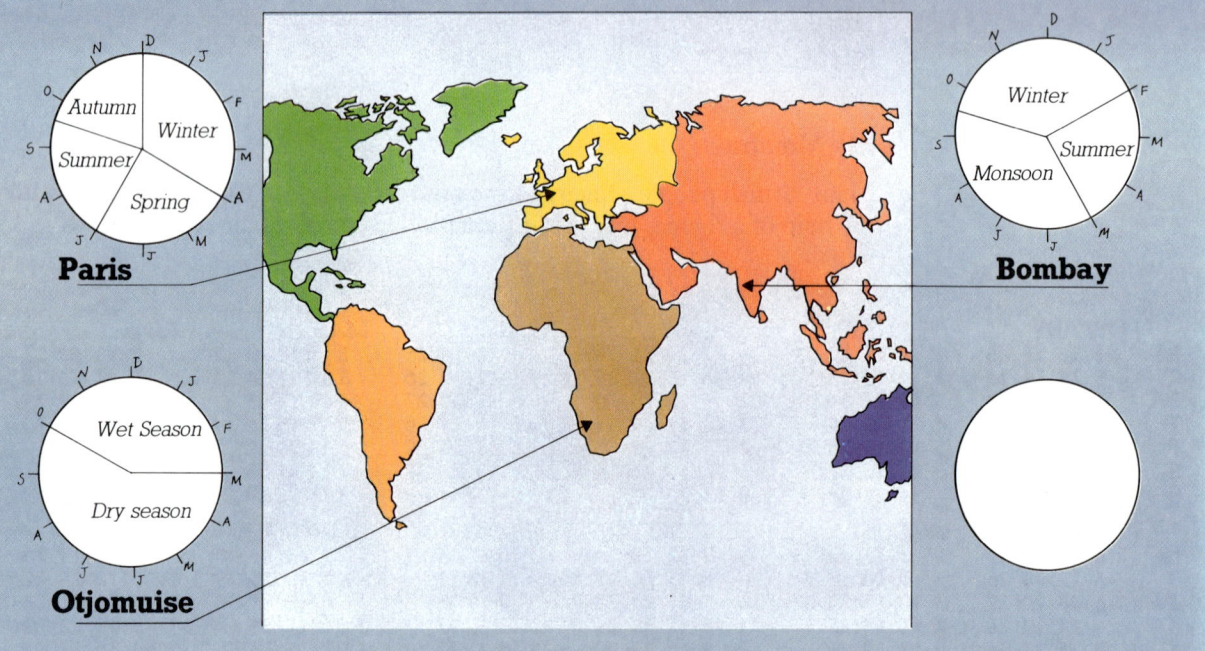

Paris (capital of France) has a temperate climate. It has four seasons: Spring, Summer, Autumn and Winter. Winters are mild – about 7°C in the daytime, and summers are warm – about 22°C. The diagram shows when the seasons are.

Otjomuise (Windhoek – capital of Namibia) has a hot climate. It has two seasons: Rainy and Dry. The rainy season is hot – over 30°C; the dry season is warm – about 20°C.

Bombay (an important Indian city) has a monsoon climate. It has three seasons: Summer is very hot around 30°C; the monsoon season is warm about 23°C and it rains all day, every day; Winter is dry and mild around 15°C.

How many seasons are there where you live? What are they?
Fill in the blank chart for your area or for a place you know.

[D] This text is just for interest.

At home... ...and abroad

FORECAST for Bangkok Metropolis until tomorrow morning: Scattered showers or thunderstorms in the afternoon and evening affecting 40 per cent of the area, south-westerly winds 10-25 kph.

Today the sun rises at 5.49 a.m., sets at 6.42 p.m., high tide at 4.58 a.m. and 9.03 p.m., low tide at 2.14 a.m. and 11.34 a.m.

Yesterday's minimum temperature 26.4C (79.5F) at 5.10 a.m., maximum temperature 33.6C (92.5F) at 1.40 p.m., average temperature 30C (86F), average humidity 72 per cent, and relative humidity at 7 p.m. 76 per cent.

Amsterdam:	12–16 C	Jakarta:	24–32 C	Seoul:	18–25 C
Athens:	14–28 C	Kuala Lumpur:	23–33 C	Singapore:	26–31 C
Bahrain:	29–37 C	London:	7–16 C	Sydney:	11–20 C
Beirut:	not available	Los Angeles:	19–35 C	Taipei:	23–27 C
Belgrade:	13–23 C	Madrid:	5–21 C	Tel Aviv:	19–27 C
Berlin:	8–16 C	Manila:	23–35 C	Tokyo:	18–22 C
Brussels:	7–18 C	Moscow:	10–17 C	Toronto:	7–10 C
Buenos Aires:	11–17 C	New Delhi:	32–44 C	Vancouver:	8–17 C
Cairo:	17–36 C	New York:	14–16 C	Vienna:	11–22 C
Copenhagen:	13–22 C	Paris:	8–14 C	Warsaw:	11–24 C
Frankfurt:	7–11 C	Peking:	17–35 C		
Geneva:	6–12 C	Rio de Janeiro:	15–33 C		
Helsinki:	12–16 C	Rome:	8–22 C		
Hong Kong:	24–25 C	San Francisco:	15–28 C		

Bangkok Post 30.5.84.

Unit 6

1 Match each picture to a definition.

can (*n*) (formerly US, now GB) Metal container for foods, liquids, etc.
can (*aux*) **1** to show ability to do something, e.g. Can you swim? Can she speak Spanish? **2** To ask for something politely, e.g. Can I have a menu, please? Can you help me with this heavy case, please? **3** To say what is possible, e.g. You can pay by American Express or Visa. Finland can be very cold in winter.

2

Pairs

Where would you hear this conversation?

Is *can* used:
to ask for something?
to show ability?
to show possibility?

A: Yes, sir?
B: Can I have a toy elephant, please?
A: Certainly. What colour do you want?
B: I, er, don't know ... Have you got a blue one?

Make 8 questions.

Can you tell me	the correct time?
	with this exercise? I don't understand it.
	fill in this form?
Can you help me	another one, please?
Can I have	the bill, please?
	the way to the post office?
	three copies of this letter, please?
	clean up the office?

Choose one of these questions. Think of a situation. Make up a short conversation like the one on the left. Write it down. Do the same for two more questions.

31

3 Here are two problems.

  a This teeshirt is covered in tomato sauce. How can you clean it?
  b This ring is stuck on his finger. How can he get it off?

  Can you think of two, three, four ... ways?

4 Ability or possibility?

Text number 3 uses *can* for 'ability'. What about the others?

[1]
DANGER: Government Health WARNING:
CIGARETTES CAN
SERIOUSLY DAMAGE YOUR HEALTH

[2]
You can pay by cheque, Access or Visa. Whichever way is most convenient for you, is fine with us.

[3]
SPY IN THE SKY
It probably can read a car number plate from 100 miles up. The trouble is that the military satellite can see altogether too much. Futures examines the information overload

Guardian 17.6.85

[4]
I.Q. of 145 and Can't Remember?

A FAMOUS international publisher reports that
is a simple technique for acquiring a powerful
ry which can pay you real dividends in both
ess and social
cement. It works
agic to give you
d poise, self-
nce and greater

ils of this
escribed in
ng book,
Memory",

lisher,
ealise
ce

Forget facts, figures?

by possessing a

5 Request or ability?

Listen to these conversations.
Three people ask for something.
Three people talk about ability.
Put a tick ✓ in one of the columns for each speaker.

	request	ability
A		
B		
C		
D		
E		
F		

Language 6

can

Form

Affirmative: Subject + can + verb *Birds can fly.*

Negative: Subject + cannot (can't) + verb *Humans can't fly.*

Interrogative: can + subject + verb *Can elephants fly?*
What can you do?

Use

1 To express ability *I can type fifty words a minute.*
2 To express possibility *We can go by car or train.*
3 To make a request *Can I have a cup of coffee, please?*

Pronunciation

In most sentences we pronounce *can* as [kən].
Practise saying: Can you ...   Can I ...
                 She can ...   We can ...

Now say: *Yes, I can.*
Here the pronunciation is [kæn]
Compare [kən] [kæn]

Adverbs

Placido Domingo is a superb singer. He sings superbly.

superb – adjective
superbly – adverb

Form

Regular
slow/slowly
quick/quickly
beautiful/beautifully

Rule: adjective + _____ = adverb

Irregular
good/well
hard/hard   *She is a fast driver.*
fast/fast   *She drives very fast.*

Write examples for *good* and *well*;
                   hard and *hard*.

Word order

Look at these examples.

He can swim really well. They dance very slowly. They work hard.
She can talk awfully quickly.

Rule: verb + | really | + _____
               | very |
               | awfully |

6

Possessive pronouns

Possessive adjectives come immediately before the noun or adjective + noun: **my** hat, **my** blue hat (see page 8).

Possessive pronouns come after the verb.
That hat is **mine.** *It's* **mine.**

Match each picture to a sentence.

1 It's mine.   5 They're theirs.
2 It's ours.   6 It's yours.
3 They're his. 7 Here are yours.
4 It's hers.

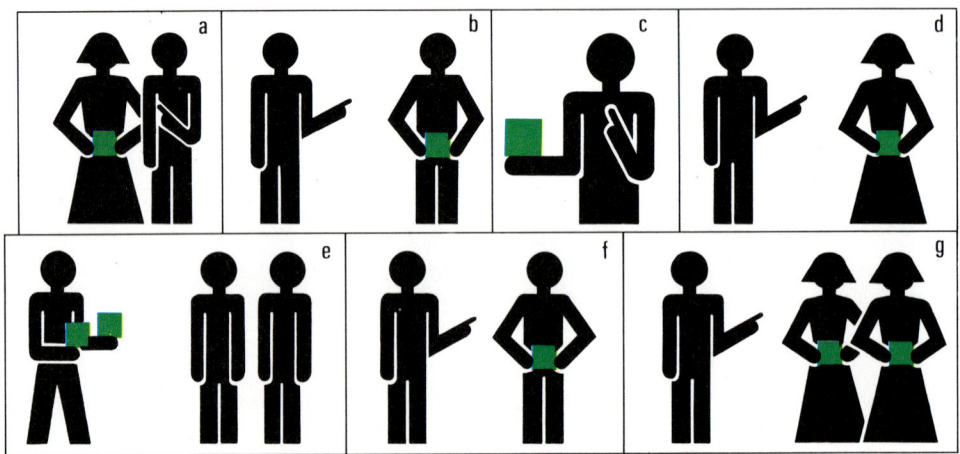

Vocabulary

Look through this unit and make a list of the words which occur frequently. Check the meaning carefully. Write example sentences.

Practice in Listening

Read the questions below. Then listen to the tape and answer the questions.

1 How old are they?
   Are they children/teenagers/young adults/middle-aged people/old people?
2 Do they know each other/not know each other?
   Do they like each other/dislike each other?
3 Are they happy?
   Are they sad?

Developments 6

Messages and signs   [A] Read these messages. Match the message to the situation.

a _____ Congratulations and best wishes. Yvonne

b _____ Back in ten minutes

c _____ Bed and Breakfast VACANCIES

d _____ Opening hours 9.30–3.30 Mon–Fri

e _____ Annie phoned. She'll phone back later.

f _____ Queue here for STAND A

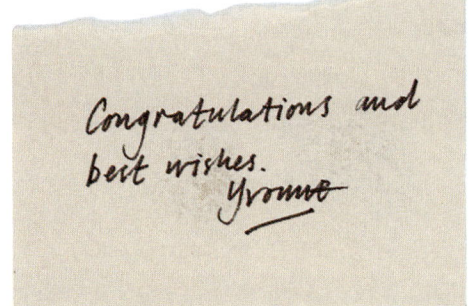
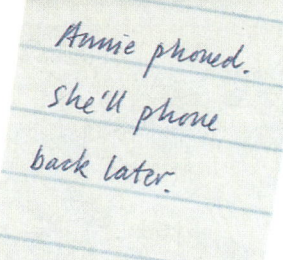

35

6

[B] (i) Listen to this telephone conversation. Choose the correct message.

a) Mary – The meeting is now at 7.00. Take your books and tapes

b) Mary – The meeting tonight is now at 7.30. Take your notes.

c) Mary – The meeting is now at 7.30. Take your books and tapes.

(ii) Listen. Choose the correct picture.

(iii) Listen. Choose the message which matches what you hear.

a) Mr Moore: Mr Rees phoned. He'll phone you back later.

b) Mr Moore: Mr Rees came in. He would like to see you as soon as possible.

c) Mr Moore: Please ring Howard Rees of Zoom Films – 2057 3161 – as soon as possible.

[C] Listen to this telephone conversation.
Complete the message to Ric's wife.

Nigel phoned. He's got four tickets for the Russian .... Can we go? It's on ...... night. We can meet in the ...... in Bridge Street at ...... o'clock. Is that okay? Please phone Nigel tonight. I'll be back late tonight. Love you.

Unit 7

1 Look at the picture. There are two people in the car. What can the people on the bank do? Listen to the tape. Do they choose to:

a Cut down a tree to fall on the roof of the car. Then people climb along the tree?
b Phone for a rescue helicopter?
c Get three ropes, tie one around one person. Swim to the car with ropes for the other people?

2 Groups

Can you think of other suggestions?

3 Groups

You are on a walk in the mountains. Suddenly you see this situation. Decide what you will do.
How many different solutions can you think of?

Useful Language

We could try ...
Why don't we get ...?
Let's give ...
That's a good idea.
No, that's no good.
We can't do that.
You're crazy, that won't work.

7

4 *What people do for their art!*

STATEMENT   July, 1983

We, LINDA MONTANO and TEHCHING HSIEH, plan to do a one year performance.
We will stay together for one year and never be alone.
We will be in the same room at the same time, when we are inside.
We will be tied together at the waist with an 8 foot rope.
We will never touch each other during the year.
The performance will begin on July 4, 1983 at 6 p.m., and continue until July 4, 1984 at 6 p.m.

Linda Montano   *Tehching Hsieh*
LINDA MONTANO   TEHCHING HSIEH

111 Hudson St, 2 Fl. New York, N.Y. 10013

Information: EXIT ART 966–7745

5 Groups

Look at these other examples of performance art.
Do these pictures give you any ideas for other, different performances?
Decide on a performance which you will do.
Decide why you will do it.
Decide on the rules for your performance.
Write a statement of your rules.

Language 7

Let's **Form**

Let us (let's) + verb *Let's phone the police.*

Use

To make a suggestion

could **Form**

We use *could* for all persons.
Subject + could + verb *We could cut the tree.*

Use

1 To make a suggestion *You could pull him up.*
2 To express possibility *We could do this or that.*
3 To make a request *Could you help?*

will **Form**

See page 27.

Use

1 To make a prediction *It'll rain tomorrow.*
2 To state plans/intentions *We will stay together.*
3 To express an instant decision *I'll write to them now.*

Prepositions of time Test yourself. How many of these prepositions of time can you match?

at, in, at, on, in, on, on, at, in, on

2 o'clock, Wednesday, the weekend, the evening, January 21st, April 1926, 1976, May Day, night, his/her birthday

Vocabulary Look at the two pictures on page 37. How many things can you label?
For example, *sky, river*, etc. Use a dictionary.

Practice in Listening

Read the questions below. Then listen to the tape and answer the questions.
a How many speakers are there?
b Are they anxious/relaxed?
c Where are they?

Developments

Airports

a Look at the arrivals board. Listen and tick ✓ the flights which you hear.
b Show where the people go. Draw an arrow.
c Fill in the destination and the flight number on the planes.

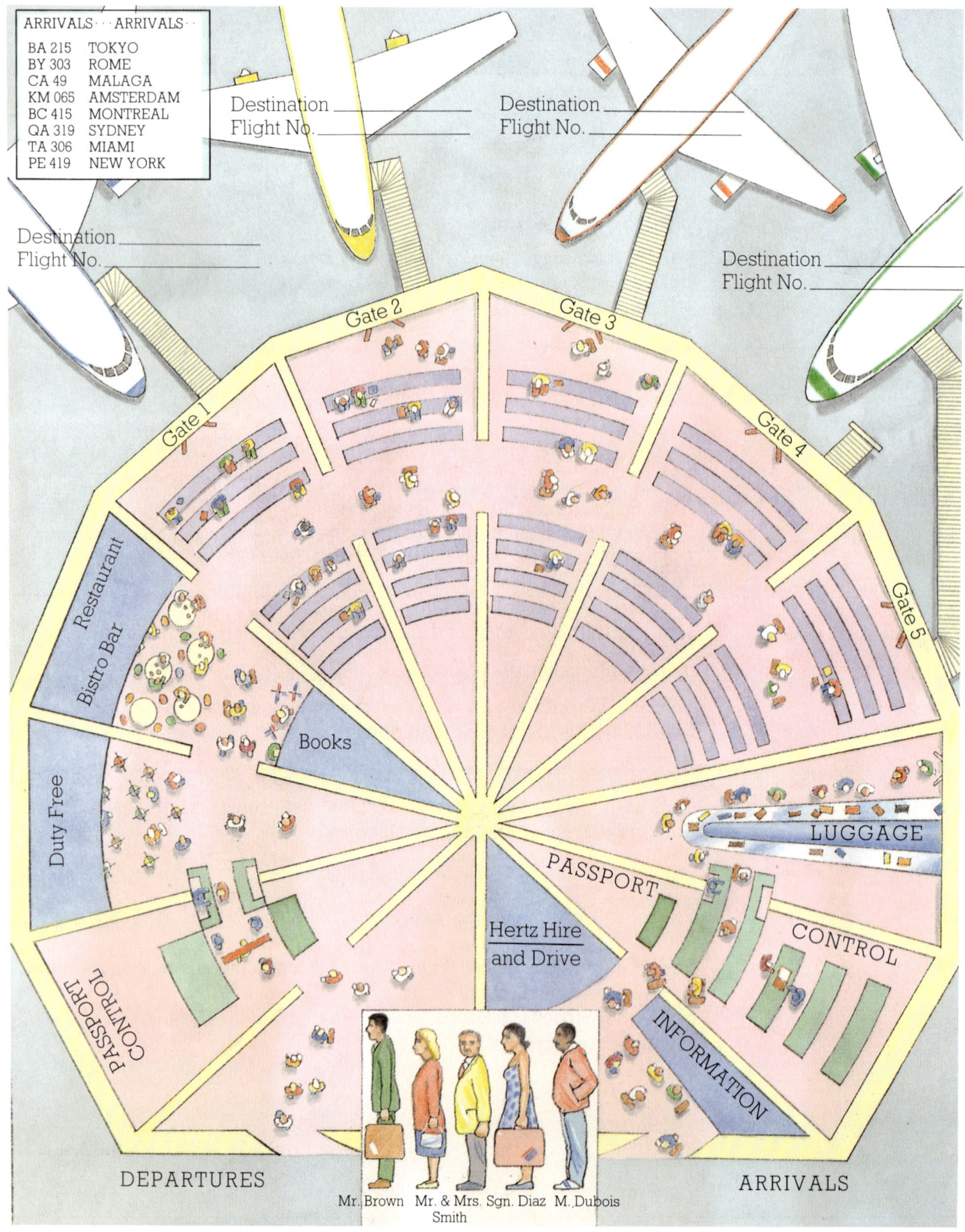

Unit 8

1 Pairs

What does it cost to run a car? List what expenses you have.

2 List the answers to these questions.

Which is the most economical car?
Which car has the smallest engine?
Which car has the biggest engine?
Which car has the fastest acceleration?
Which car has the highest top speed?

	0–90 Kph	Max speed	Engine Size	Litre per 100 Km.
Austin Metro	16.5 secs	134 Kph	998 cc	7.4
Renault 5 TL	18.4 secs	128 Kph	1108 cc	7.6
Fiat Strada TC	9.4 secs	169 Kph	1585 cc	8.9
Citroën 2CV	30.9 secs	108 Kph	602 cc	5.7
Golf GTi	8.4 secs	179 Kph	1781 cc	8.8
Datsun 280 ZX Coupé	9.0 sec	194 Kph	2753 cc	9.8

3 Pairs

Choose one of the cars. Compare it with the one your partner chooses.

Which car is	bigger?	Which car is	more expensive?
	cheaper to run?		more attractive?
	faster?		more comfortable?
	easier to drive?		more practical?

4 Pairs

[A] Look at these statements. Listen and ✓ tick the correct ones.

a The Burtons drive a new car/an old car
                use their car for local travel/long distance travel
                want a bigger/smaller car
                want a car which is cheaper to run

A dealer offers them the choice of:
    a four-year-old Golf GTi for £2,900
or an 18-month-old Metro for £3,200.
Decide which is the best car for the Burtons and say why.

b Jim Lodge drives a sports car/family car
                uses his car for local travel/long distance travel
                wants a faster car/a slower car
                want a car which is cheaper to run

A dealer offers him the choice of:
    a two-year-old Golf GTi for £4,000,
    a one-year-old Fiat Strada for £4,200
or a four-year-old Datsun 280 ZX for £4,300.
Decide which is the best car for him and say why.

c Jenny Monroe wants a simple/luxury car
                uses her car for local travel/long distance travel
                wants a car with two doors/four doors
                wants a fast car
                wants an economical car

A dealer offers her the choice of:
    a two-year-old Renault 5GTL for £2,200
or a one-year-old Citroen 2CV for £2,500.
Decide which is the best car for her and say why.

[B] Listen again. Which cars do the Burtons, Jim Lodge and Jenny Monroe choose?

Useful Language

The ... is a good car but the ... is better.
I agree it is fast but the ... is more economical.
I think the ... is the best car for them.
Why?

Because the ... is a sports car and they want a family car.
The ... is too expensive to run.
The ... isn't economical.
The ... is too old. It'll cost a lot to service.

50 designer cars made for women

The fashion designer Zandra Rhodes is producing a limited edition of cars for women which will have 'lots of space for rubbish'. The fifty Renault 5's will be shocking pink and be signed on the bonnet. They will have practical things that Miss Rhodes says women look for in a car. These will include designer overalls, tools covered in pink plastic, a mirror on the driver's sun visor and somewhere to put the rubbish.

Mr David Mattia, an Aldershot Renault dealer will sell the cars in the autumn. 'The cars are for adventurous career women with a design flair,' says Mr Mattia. 'Women now buy a quarter of all private cars sold.'

A survey by Mr Mattia of 200 male and female car owners shows that women see their car as a vehicle designed to transport them from A to B and that they use the inside as a mobile shopping basket or briefcase. 'Men are more personally attached to their car and see it as a part of themselves,' says Mr Mattia.

Adapted from an article in *The Times* 9.7.84.

Glossary (A glossary helps you to read. Do NOT learn these words.)

(to) produce – to make or create something
a limited edition – a small number; there will only be fifty of these cars
Aldershot – a town in SE England
adventurous – to like strange, exciting or unusual things
a career woman with design flair – a professional woman, e.g. a lawyer, teacher, etc., who wants good design
a vehicle – cars, buses, motorbikes, lorries, etc. are all vehicles
(to be) personally attached to – to have strong feelings for an object; to love something, e.g. a car

Groups

The article makes suggestions about car design.

[A] Discuss the ideas on:
   The colour
   The overalls
   The mirror
   The tools

Will women like them? Will men? Do you like these ideas?

[B] Discuss the ideas in the article about men and cars.
   Discuss the ideas in the article about women and cars.

How do you think men see cars?
How do you think women see cars?
Do you think the two sexes see cars differently? Or is it personal?

Language

Comparatives and superlatives of adjectives

	Comparative	*Superlative*
(i)	adjective + *er* (+ *than*)*	the + adjective + *est*
	cheaper (*than*)*	the cheapest
(ii)	*more* + adjective (+ *than*)*	the + *most* + adjective
	more expensive (*than*)*	the most expensive

*optional

For short adjectives (all one-syllable and some two-syllable adjectives) we use form (i).
For long adjectives (most two-syllable and all three-syllable adjectives) we use form (ii).
For all adjectives with *ed* at the end we use form (ii): *tired, bored*.

Pronunciation: ... than [ðən]

Practise saying: cheaper than that; quicker than that; bigger than that.

Examples

Superlatives

The red car | is / isn't | the | oldest / most economical | one.

Write 4 sentences from the information in this table.

Comparatives

The blue one | is / isn't | cheaper / more expensive | than the white one.

Write 4 sentences.

Questions: Comparatives and Superlatives

Which one is | quicker than that one?
            | the most attractive?
Is this one | more economical than that one?
            | the cheapest?

Write 8 questions.

Note: Good and *bad* are irregular adjectives.

	Comparative	*Superlative*
good	better	best
bad	worse	worst

Vocabulary

Make a list of all the adjectives you can find in this unit. Check the meaning.
What things can be described by each adjective?
For example, *high* – mountains/prices/costs/clouds.

Practice in Listening

Listen to these three conversations.
Where are they?
Which adjective describes each woman?
very friendly   polite   rude

Developments 8

[A]

There are many world records. How many things can you identify as 'Firsts'? *The first plane in the world.*

How many superlatives can you identify? *The world's tallest man.*

8

[B]

Think of five countries or cities you want to visit. Find the cheapest and most expensive flights to those places.

What do you think 'o/w' and 'rtn' mean?

Find the cheapest coach trip to Venice.
How many agencies offer cheap flights to Canada?
Find an agency which offers camping holidays in Morocco.
Which do you think is the best trip? Why?
Write 2 to 4 sentences to explain why. Begin, 'I think the ... trip is the best because ...'

Unit 9

1 Look at the two pictures. Picture 1 is all 'stuff'. Picture 2 is all 'things'. What is the difference between stuff and things? Can you add to these pictures?
Look at the rule on page 50.

9

2 We use the expressions 'things' and 'stuff' when:
1 we don't know the name, i.e. the noun;
2 when it is not important.

Look at the collage. Mark all the 'things' with a 't' and all the 'stuff' with an 's'. Do not try to name the pictures.

3 Pairs
You have one minute. Make two lists:
a of all the countable nouns (things) that you know;
b of all the uncountable nouns (stuff) that you know.
Compare your lists with others.

4 Are these countable or uncountable?
knowledge, ideas, stupidity, kisses, a brain, understanding
Are they countable or uncountable in your language?

5 Pairs/Groups

You are an English teacher. How can you show this class that *books*, *clothes*, *people*, etc. are all countable and *oil*, *sand*, *grass*, etc. are all uncountable. Note two or three ideas for a lesson.

6 [A] Look at the collage again. Find out the name for each item.

[B] Pairs

Look at the items in the collage.

How | much is / many are | there in each picture?

How *much* water |is| there?   How *many* ants |are| there?
there |is| there |are|
└─────LOTS─────┘

Pronunciation

Practise saying:
There's lot‿sof...
There's masse‿sof...

[C] Specific quantities

A pile of flour

Two kilos of flour

What can we use for:
milk   rice?

7 Listen. In each conversation there is a question about quantity.
Write the question.

1 at home _____?
2 in the living room _____?
3 before a meeting _____?
4 at the end of the meeting _____?

Language

Uncountables (mass nouns) and countables (count nouns)

	UNCOUNTABLE 'stuff'		COUNTABLE 'things'
there is	masses of / a lot of / some / a little / a bit of	there are	masses of / a lot of / some / a few / a couple of
there isn't	any / much	there aren't	any / many
is there	any? / a lot? / much?	are there	any? / a lot? / many?
Yes, there is. No, there isn't (any).		Yes, there are. No, there aren't (any).	

too/enough

[A] Look at these problems. Which of the statements is/are correct for 1, 2, and 3?

1 I want to buy that. I've got £300.
   a I've got enough money.
   b I've got more than enough.
   c It's too expensive.

2 I want to mend that wall.
   a There are probably enough.
   b There are far too many.
   c There aren't enough.

3 I want to fill this container to the line.
   a There's probably enough.
   b That's too much.
   c There isn't enough.

[B] Give two answers to each question.

 Why can't he reach the shelf?   Because he isn't tall enough.
　　　　　　　　　　　　　　　　　　　　　　　　Because it's too high.

 Why can't she drive?   Because _____
　　　　　　　　　　　　　　　　　　　　　Because _____

 Why can't it go through?   Because _____
　　　　　　　　　　　　　　　　　　　　　　Because _____

 Why can't he lift it?   Because _____
　　　　　　　　　　　　　　　　　　　　Because _____

Vocabulary   Look through this unit (pages 47–52) and list ten words you want to learn. Choose the words which interest you; the ones which are useful to you. Check the meaning in a dictionary. Write one sentence with each word.

Practice in Listening

Listen to the conversations.

How many speakers are there on each tape?
Which conversation is formal?
Where are they?

Developments

[A]

Peter and Michael live in a flat in London. Michael telephones Peter and asks him to do some shopping.

Listen to the phone call.
1 Note down all the things Michael needs for dinner.
2 Check the cupboard and the fridge.
3 Write a shopping list.

[B]

We buy cream in cartons – so we say 'a carton of cream'.
We buy spaghetti in packets.
We buy fruit and vegetables fresh, frozen or in tins.
Look at the cupboard and the fridge.
Make a list of all the packets, tins, and cartons.

These are all 'containers'.
What other containers are there in the fridge and cupboard?

[C]

Listen to the tape again. Note down all the expressions of quantity, e.g. *some*.

Unit 10

1 The map shows the twenty-four World Time Zones. These are divided by 15° (degree) lines of longitude.

Find the 0° longitude.
Find the 180° longitude.
What are these two lines called?

Look at this sentence:
When it's 12.00 am in London, it's 7.00 am in New York.

When it's 3.00 pm in Paris, what time is it in San Francisco?
When it's 9.00 pm in Hong Kong, what time is it in Rome?

Think of other examples and question other people.

2 Here are some facts. Can you match the cause with the effect?

If you live in the far north	your heart beats more quickly.
If you hold your nose and eat cucumber and potato	you move forward in time.
	it dissolves.
When you touch a lighted match	you burn yourself.
If you put a coconut in water	you get orange.
When you run very fast for some time	it floats.
	you have no daylight in winter.
If you mix red and yellow	you cannot taste the difference.
When you travel East from London	
If you put sugar in hot water	

10

3 Complete these sentences. Look back at page 24 if you wish.

If the sun warms water _____
When air becomes warm _____
If moist air becomes colder _____

4 Superstitions

Some people believe that if you break a mirror it brings bad luck for seven years; that if a black cat crosses in front of you it brings good luck; that if you walk under a ladder you must cross your fingers.

Groups
Find out how many people in the group are superstitious. Make a list of all the different superstitions you can think of.

Class
Collect all the superstitions. Divide them into groups – by countries/areas and by good/bad luck. Check the words you don't know in a dictionary.

Useful Language
Are you superstitious?
What do you do if you walk under a ladder?
I believe/think that if . . .
Do you really believe that . . . ?

5 Research shows that very successful language learners do some or all of the following things:

Find a good way to learn. There are many ways to learn a language and *different* people learn in *different* ways.

Try to 'be' a native speaker. A good student of French tries to think and speak as a French person.

Practise a lot; talk to native speakers, listen to the radio, watch films and buy newspapers.

Try to understand the meaning of what people say but don't worry about every word. When you don't know the meaning of individual words, guess!

Learn the 'systems'. All languages have 'systems', i.e. patterns and tenses.

Experiment. Try to find new rules and systems.

Ask the teacher for help. But remember the teacher can only help; s/he cannot learn for you.

Remember – making mistakes is an important part of learning a language. If you relax it is easier to understand and speak. You must not worry.

Learn from your mistakes and have fun!

Groups
Look at each idea.
Which do *you* do?
Is this information useful?
Do you think any of these ideas are 'silly'?
Which of these do you think you must do?
Can you think of any other ideas?
Will this information change the way you study?

Language   10

'0' Conditional

Condition   *Result*
If you put ice in the sun ...   ... it melts.
When you put water in the fridge ...   ... it freezes.

Form

If you do 'X', 'Y' happens.
or
'Y' happens if you do 'X'.
We can use *if* or *when*: When you do 'X', 'Y' happens.

Use

1 To talk about facts *If you travel west, you move backward in time.*
2 To talk about beliefs *If you spill salt, it's unlucky.*

must

Form

Affirmative: Subject + must + verb *You must experiment.*
Negative: Subject + must + not (mustn't) + verb *You mustn't forget.*

Use

It is very important to understand that *must* and *mustn't* have very different meanings/uses. *Mustn't* is not always the negative meaning of *must*.

1 *must* – for necessity *You must use a language if you want to learn it.*

2 *must not (mustn't)* – for not allowed/no permission/not advisable
   You mustn't talk loudly in a library.
   You mustn't worry if you make mistakes.

Write four realistic sentences using *must* for necessity.
And another four using *must not* for not allowed/not advisable.

Pronunciation

mustn't is pronounced [mʌsnt]

Contractions

We use a lot of contractions in English. These are some of the ones you will find:

1 In negative sentences – the auxiliary with *not*

do not – don't
have not – haven't
cannot – _____
will not – _____
is not – _____
does not – _____
are not – _____
has not – _____

10

2 The subject with the verbs *to be* and *to have*

I am hungry – I'm hungry
He has got flu – He's got flu
She is angry – _____
They are happy – _____
I have got a cold – _____
We have got three children – _____
You are clever – _____

You can only contract subject + verb if another word or words follow,
e.g. You must **not** say: ~~Yes, you're~~. You must say: *Yes, you are*.
      You can say: *No, you don't* because *not* is another word.
      You can say: *Yes, I'm hungry* because *hungry* is another word.

Tick √ the correct answers to these questions (there is more than one for each):

Do you watch TV?   **a** Yes, I do.
                     b No, I don't.
                     c Yes I'd
                     d Yes, I watch a lot.

Have you got a video? **a** No, I haven't.
                       b Yes I've
                       c Yes, I have.
                       d Yes, I've got one.

Note: Contractions are part of normal spoken English. In formal written English use the full form.

Vocabulary Look through this unit and make a list of the words which occur frequently. Check the meaning carefully. Write example sentences.

Practice in Listening

a How many voices are there?
b Are they excited?/calm?
c Choose the picture which matches what you hear.

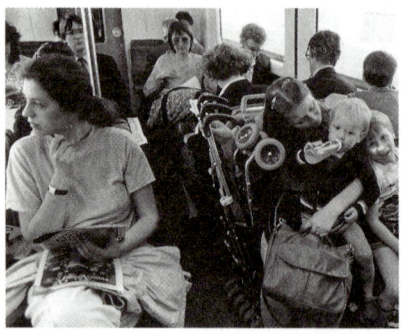  

Developments 10

[A]

Listen. Where do they put the furniture, etc? Which picture is correct?

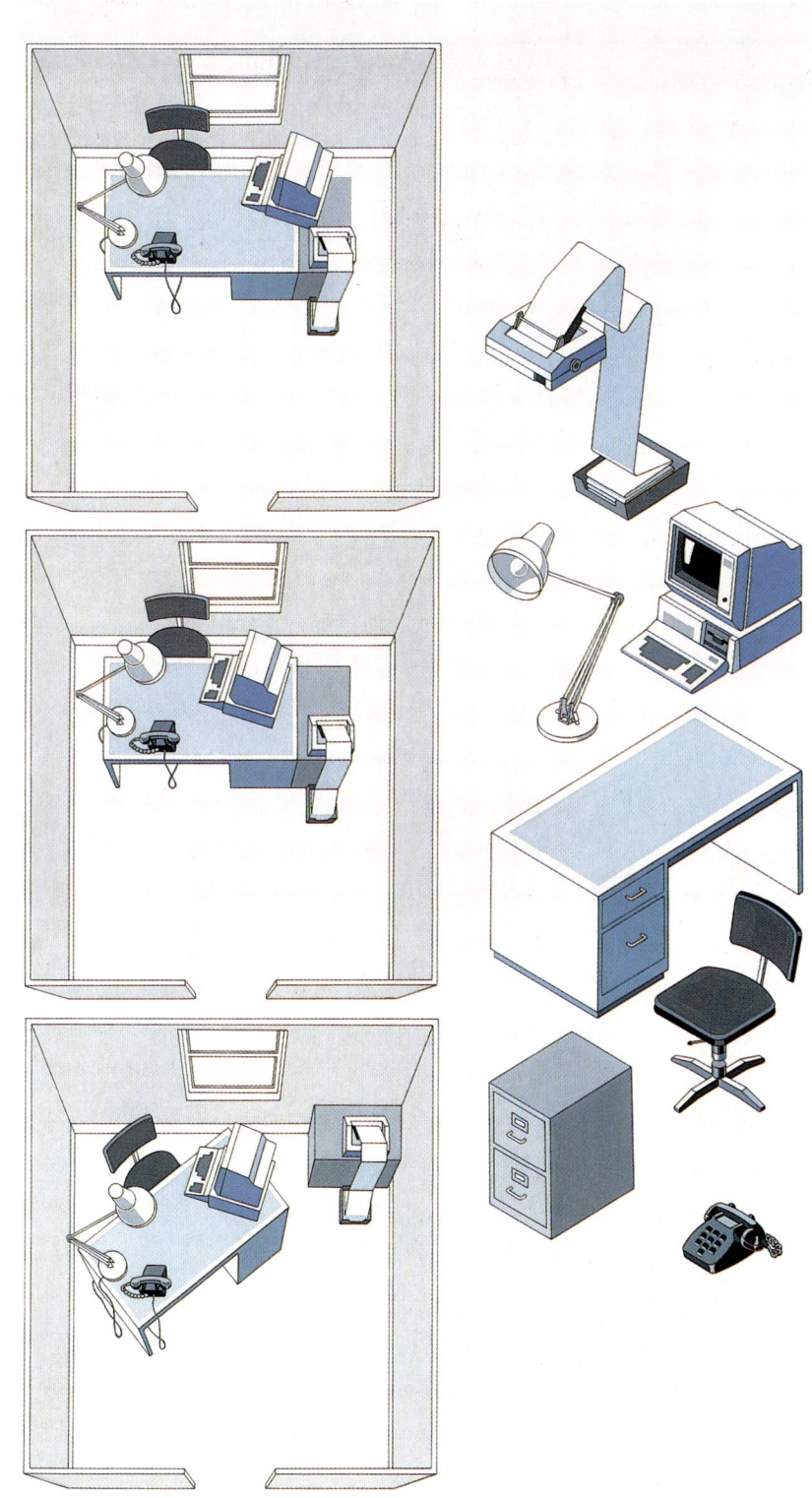

10

[B] In a dictionary:

Headwords = the words in **bold** on the left. They are in alphabetical order.

pl. = plural   *n.* = noun   *v.* = verb.   *adj.* = adjective

Look at this excerpt from the *Oxford Elementary Learner's Dictionary of English*.

a How many headwords are adjectives? List them.
b How many meanings are there for *master* (*n.*)?
c Which word has the same form when it is a noun and when it is an adjective?
d What is the adjective for *marry*?
e List the nouns which add *es* to make plurals.
f Find a word which rhymes with cat.
g Find the word which means a type of jam.
h Where can you see a mast?
i Find a word which means very large.
j Find a word which means something to hide your face.

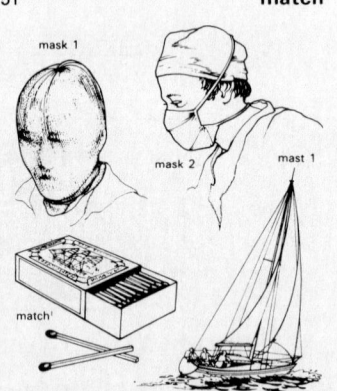

market /'mɑːkɪt/ *n.* group of shops or pens in the open air where people go to buy and sell goods: *There is a cattle market in the middle of town every Friday.* **be on the market**, be for sale: *There is a new sort of record-player on the market.*
marmalade /'mɑːməleɪd/ *n.* (no *pl.*) orange jam that British people eat at breakfast.
marrow /'mærəʊ/ *n.* sort of vegetable.
marry /'mærɪ/ *v.* **1** take someone as a husband or wife: *Samuel is going to marry my sister.* **2** join a man and woman as husband and wife: *The priest married Derek and Jane last month.* **get married**, marry: *Sue and Mike got married last month.* **married** *adj.* /'mærɪd/.
marriage /'mærɪdʒ/ *n.* time when a man and a woman are married.
marsh /mɑːʃ/ *n.* (*pl.* marshes) wet, soft ground.
marvel /'mɑːvl/ *n.* wonder; wonderful and surprising happening or person: *It's a marvel that you weren't killed in the car crash!* **marvel** *v.* (*pres. part.* marvelling, *past part. & past tense* marvelled /'mɑːvld/) be very surprised: *We marvelled at his excellent piano playing.*
marvellous /'mɑːvələs/ *adj.* wonderful; that pleases and surprises very much. **marvellously** *adv.*
masculine /'mæskjʊlɪn/ *adj.* of or like a man; right for a man. **masculine** *n.* word for a male or a man: *'Prince' is the masculine of 'princess'.*
mash /mæʃ/ *v.* crush or squash food to make it soft.
mask /mɑːsk/ *n.* **1** cover that you put over the face to hide it: *The thief was wearing a mask.* **2** covering for the face to stop gas, smoke, or germs. **mask** *v.* cover the face with a mask.
mass /mæs/ *n.* (*pl.* masses) crowd; many things or people together: *There were masses of dark clouds in the sky.*
massacre /'mæsəkə(r)/ *v.* kill a big group of people in a cruel way. **massacre** *n.*
massive /'mæsɪv/ *adj.* very big and heavy: *We needed six men to lift the massive table.*
mast /mɑːst/ *n.* **1** tall, straight piece of wood or metal that stands on a boat to hold the sails, flag, etc. **2** very tall, steel post to send out radio or television signals.
master[1] /'mɑːstə(r)/ *n.* **1** chief man; head of the family. **2** male teacher: *Mr. Davies is our maths master.* **3** male owner of a horse, dog, etc. **4** expert; someone who is the best in his sort of work: *Rembrandt was a master of painting.* **5** title for a boy: *Master John Smith is seven years old.*
master[2] *v.* learn how to do something: *You will soon master French when you live in Paris.*
masterpiece /'mɑːstəpiːs/ *n.* very good piece of work; fine piece of writing, music, painting, etc.
mat /mæt/ *n.* small piece of covering for the floor: *Wipe your feet on the door mat before you go in.*
match[1] /mætʃ/ *n.* (*pl.* matches) special small stick that makes fire when you rub it on a rough place: *He struck a match to light his cigarette.*
match[2] *n.* (*pl.* matches) **1** game between two people or teams: *a boxing match; a football match.* **2** someone who is as strong, clever, etc. as another. **meet your match**, find someone who is as good as, or better than, you in a sport, etc.: *Roy was the best tennis player until he met his match in Barry.* **3** something that is the same shape, colour, size, etc. **be a good match**, be nearly the same colour, etc. as each other: *Ruth's skirt and blouse are a good match.*

Unit 11

1

Reproduced by courtesy of the Trustees, The National Gallery, London

A Scene on the Ice Near a Town by Hendrick Avercamp. (1585–1634)
This painting hangs in the National Gallery in London.
It is remarkable for its fine detail, showing many different activities.

Make a list of all the different activities:
A woman is sitting in a boat.
Some people are skating.

2
Listen.

What is the speaker talking about?
What is he doing?

3
Do you eat breakfast? What do you eat for breakfast? How do you prepare breakfast? What things do you do?

Now listen. Say what s/he is doing.

11

4

Japanese Micro-chip Factory Creates 100 New Jobs.

Standard of Living Falls as Inflation Tops 10%...

Word Processors – Do They Cause Health Problems?

Automation Brings Job Losses in Car Industry

Groups

Think about jobs.
Are computers/robots/electronic systems changing your work?
How are these things changing your society?
Are they putting people out of work or creating new jobs?

Think about your standard of living.
Is it rising or falling?
Why?
What about the cost of living?

Useful Language

In my country/area . . .
Things are changing very fast/slowly.
More and more people are . . .
Employment/unemployment is rising/falling . . .
The cost of living is . . .
Prices are going up and up.

5

Eustace: What are you doing?
Lucinda: I'm packing.
Eustace: Why?
Lucinda: Because I'm leaving.
Eustace: You're not.
Lucinda: Yes, I am. I'm catching the first train tomorrow.
Eustace: But, but . . .
Lucinda: . . . and I'm not coming back.
Eustace: Oh, oh . . . where are you going?
Lucinda: To . . . to . . . uh, Hawaii.
Eustace: Oh darling.

6

Pairs

Imagine Lucinda telephones Eustace two weeks later. Write a similar dialogue . . . but this time Lucinda is coming back.

Language 11

Present Continuous

Form

Subject + to be + present participle (verb + *ing*)

Affirmative: Subject + | am (I'm) / is (He's) / are (They're) | + verb + *ing*. | *We're working in Montreal now.*

Negative: Subject + | am / is / are | + not (isn't) (aren't) + verb + *ing*. | *They aren't working tomorrow.*

Interrogative: am / is / are | + subject + verb + *ing*. | *Is he working? Where is he working?*

Use

1 To talk about something that is happening now . . . *and Black Knight's leading the race.*
2 To describe the actions in a picture, photo, etc. *They're skating.*
3 To talk about something that is happening for a limited time *I'm living in Paris at the moment. Society is changing.*
4 To talk about something definite in the near future *I'm travelling to Rome next week; I've got the tickets in my pocket.*

Present time

We use both Present Continuous and Simple Present to talk about present time, but they each mean something different.
Remember we use the Simple Present to talk about facts, regular habits, processes, routines, feelings and thoughts. See page 21.
For uses of the Present Continuous see above.

Simple Present or Present Continuous?

Which of these sentences are correct? Correct the ones that are wrong.
1 The sun is rising every day.
2 I'm reading a good book by Alice Walker.
3 I like the picture by Avercamp very much.
4 Water is usually condensing in cold air.
5 The standard of living rises at the moment.

Spelling: present participle

A verb has several forms:
to walk – infinitive
walk – base verb
walking – present participle

How do we form the present participle?

1 These are correct:
walk – walking   think – thinking
try – trying   open – opening
go – going   listen – listening

Complete the rule: Take the base _____ and add _____.

61

11

2 So are these:

sho<u>p</u>	shopping
ref<u>e</u>r	referring
r<u>u</u>n	running
sw<u>i</u>m	swimming
perm<u>i</u>t	permitting

Rule: For verbs ending consonant-verb-consonant with stress on the last syllable, double the last _____ and _____ _____

3 So are these:

continue	–	continuing
make	–	making
hope	–	hoping
drive	–	driving
argue	–	arguing
leave	–	leaving

Rule: For verbs which end in -*e* drop the _____ and _____ _____

Note: If there are two -*e*'s, e.g. see/seeing, do not drop the *e*.

Vocabulary   Check you understand the words below. Use a dictionary. Find one example of each in Unit 11.

a painting, an activity, a speaker, unemployment, to happen, to talk about, to leave, the cost of living, the standard of living, syllable, stress

Practice in Listening

Match the picture to the conversation.

 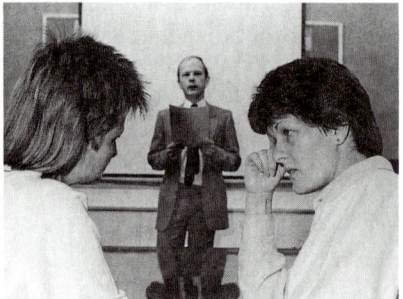 

Listen again.

1 – Is the listener bored or interested?
2 – Is the speaker happy or sad?
3 – Do they know each other?

62

Developments 11

Stations These are station announcements. Listen to the tape and fill in the blanks in the picture.

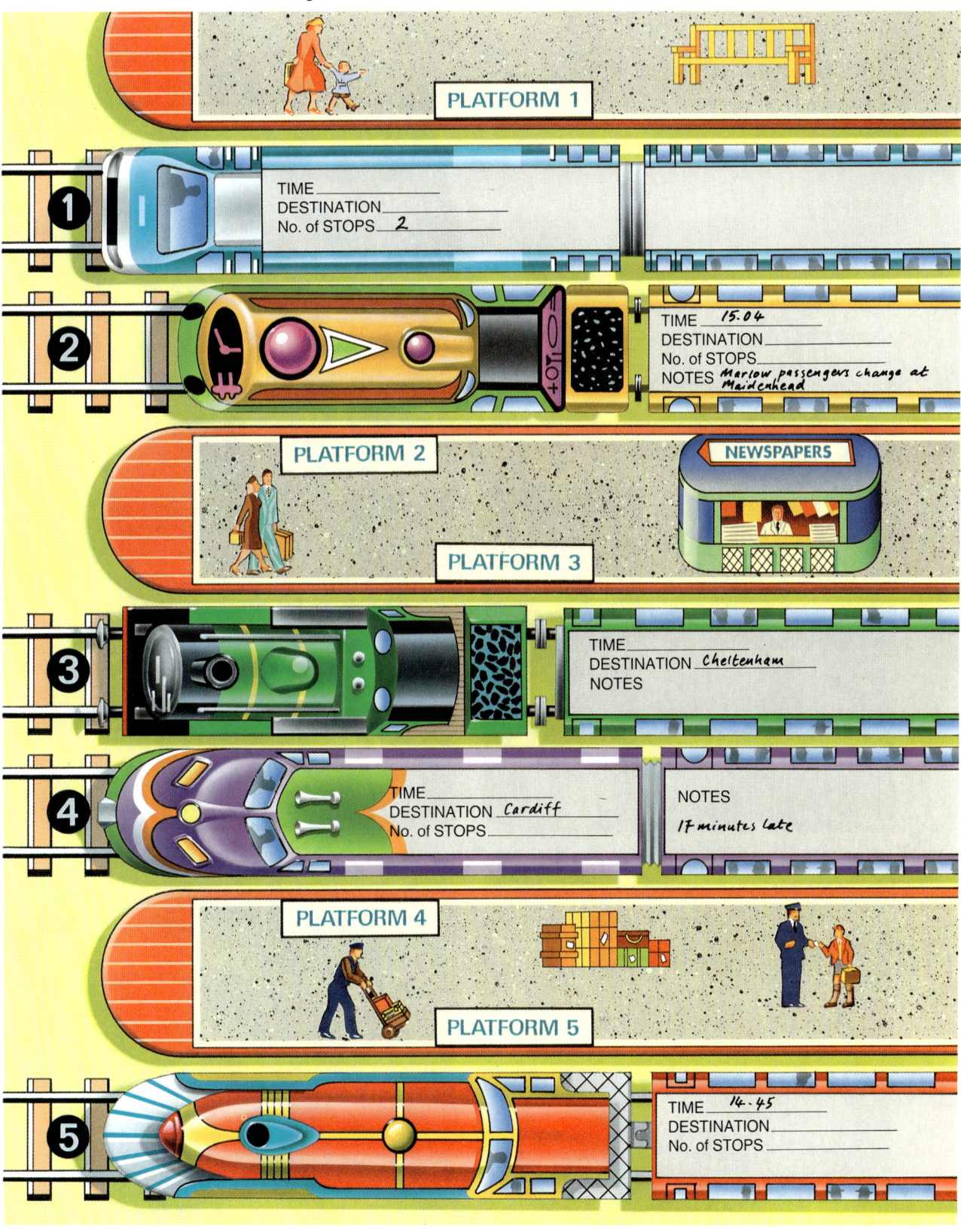

Unit 12

1 Can you identify these places – The name?
The country? The continent?

Listen.
Place _____?
Which place is each speaker talking about?

Listen again.
Reason _____?
Business or pleasure?

Listen again.
Time _____?
Are they there now?

Pronunciation

Listen to the pronunciation of these words:
was; wasn't.
In normal speech we pronounce these:
[wəz] [wəznt]
In short answers: *Yes, I was. No, he wasn't!*
We pronounce these: [wɒz] [wɒznt]

12

2 This picture shows the funeral of a famous woman.
Who was this woman?
What country was she from?
What was her job?
Was the event important? Why?
When was it?
Where was it?

3 This is an exercise to practise *was/were* questions.
There are two pictures on pages 134 and 136.
These are pictures of important world events.

Pairs

Partner A: On page 134 you will find a picture. Do not tell B what is in your picture. Decide what the event was, who the people were, when the event was and why it was important. Do not speak. B must ask questions and find out what your event was. Answer their questions with *yes, no, maybe, I don't know* and *it's not important*.

Partner B: Find out the event in A's picture. Ask questions with *was* and *were*,
e.g. *Was it last year?*
Was it outside?
Were there a lot of people?

Change over. A ask the questions about B's event.

Now think of recent important national or international events.
Do the same exercise again with your events.

Language

was/were: the past tense of to be

Form

Affirmative: Subject + | was / were | *I was in Quito.*

Negative: Subject + | was not (wasn't) / were not (weren't) | *She wasn't French.*

Interrogative: | was / were | + subject + there? | *Were you there? / When were you there?*

Use

The verb *to be* in the past
I'm hungry.   I *was* hungry.
They're here today.   They *were* here yesterday.

Past time adverbials

What is the date today? Put the correct date/s beside each expression.

yesterday _____   the day before yesterday _____

yesterday | morning _____ / afternoon _____ / evening _____

the week / the month / the year | before last | _____

last | night _____ / weekend _____ / week _____ / month _____ / year _____

last | Monday _____ / Tuesday _____ / January _____ / February _____

Note: the other day = recently
a few days ago = recently

at the weekend | *She was there at the weekend.*   PAST TIME
| *I'll be there at the weekend.*   FUTURE TIME

'What was it like?'

This is an idiom. It is a question asking for a description.
What was the weather like? ▷ It was hot and sunny.
What is she like?   ▷ She's very friendly.
What's that book like?   ▷ It's very good.

Look at these questions and answers.
Tick √ the possible answers and cross X the wrong ones.

What is Barcelona like?   It's a great city.
                          I like Spain.
                          Hundreds of tourists and lots to see.

What was the film like?   I like the cinema.
                          It was very funny.
                          The acting was terrific.
                          I often go to the cinema.

Write answers to these questions:
What's your traditional food like? What's your home town like?

Vocabulary

Look at one of the pictures of places on page 64. How many features can you name? For example, *buildings*, *trees*.

Practice in Listening

Listen.
Which recording is enthusiastic?
Which is aggressive?
Which is peaceful?

Match the recordings to the pictures.

Developments

[A] Match each question to the best answer.

1 Can you help me?
2 What's your Dad like?
3 Can you send me some information about the school?
4 So what do you do next?
5 Where's she living now?
6 What does this do?
7 When are you coming back?
8 Have you got the time?

a It starts the machine.
b He's tall and skinny; he's quiet, doesn't talk a lot.
c Yes, of course, just give me your name and address.
d Oh, perhaps next week.
e I'll try. What's the problem?
f Yes, it's about 11.00.
g Me? Get a new job I think.
h I think she's in Spain.

[B] Listen to these six conversations. Where do you think you hear them?

Write the number of the conversation in the box:

☐ in a hotel   ☐ in an airport   ☐ at home
☐ in a train station ☐ in a car   ☐ at work

[C] Words

1 Word groups

Complete the groups of words from the list. Write in the bubbles. Add more bubbles in each group. Write more words in the bubbles.

car, house, bus, computer programmer, cinema, cashier, bicycle, writer, astronaut, train, office block, shuttle, mechanic, garage, bank, porter, station, plane

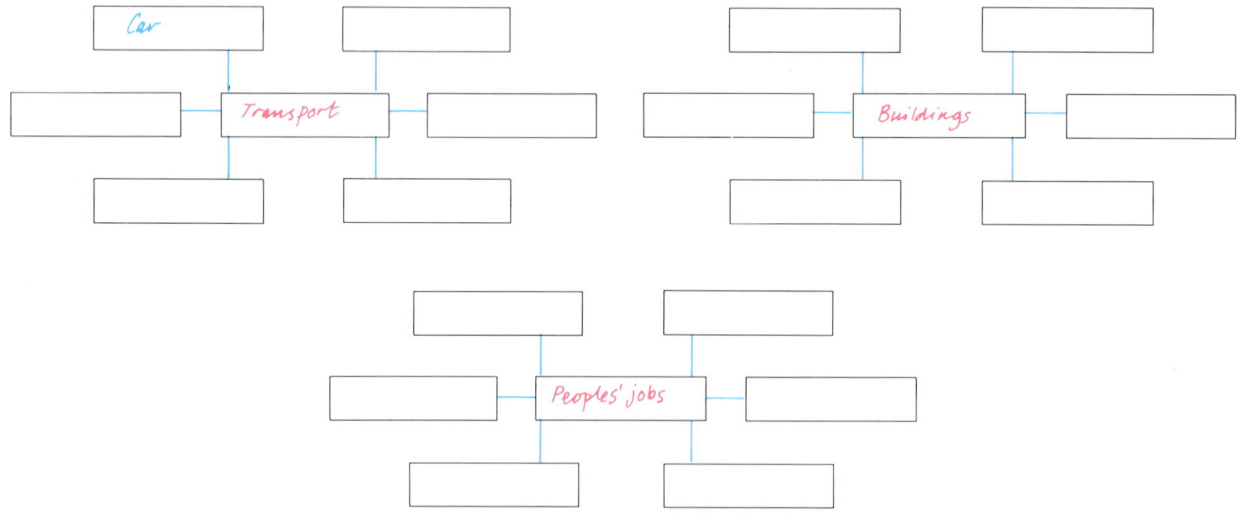

Pronunciation

Mark the stress (underline) on the following words. Check in the dictionary.

computer programmer, cinema, cashier, bicycle, writer, astronaut, mechanic, garage, porter, station, transport, buildings

68

2 Odd One Out

Identify the odd word in each group.
Example: *apple, orange,* **lettuce**, *banana, pear.*

a to run, to walk, to sit, to think, to swim.
b happy, enthusiastic, quickly, anxious, sad.
c to believe, to study, to eat, to understand, to know.
d desk, cup, chair, cupboard, table.

Give opposites for:

wet   anxious   quickly   expensive   cool   large

[D] How Many People Speak English?

Probably about 1 billion people speak English. They do not all use it as their first language. In some countries, for example, Nigeria, Burma and India, there are often many different languages and so these countries use English as an 'official' or 'second' language for government, business and education. Throughout the world many people use English as an international language: some use it for social purposes, others for business or study. A French tourist uses English on holiday in New Zealand. A Japanese businessman uses English to talk to business people all over the world. A Spanish student reads technical or scientific books in English. Finally there are the 'English-speaking countries' where most but not all people speak English as their first language.

a In line 1 'they' =
   the people who speak English
   all the people in the world
   all English people

b In line 3 'these countries' =
   India, Nigeria, and Burma
   all the countries where people speak English
   all the countries which use English as a second language

c Draw an arrow → to the word/s understood:
   For 'it' in line 1
   For 'it' in line 6

For example: Basque is very different from other European languages. ⟶It is one of the oldest languages in the world.

d In line 10 'their' =
   the inhabitants of English-speaking countries
   the majority of the inhabitants of English-speaking countries
   the majority of English-speaking people

Unit 13

1 Simple Past

[A] You know the Simple Present (see page 21):
the question form ▷ *Do you like football?*
the negative form ▷ *I don't like football.*
the short answers ▷ *Yes, I do. No, I don't.*

To form the Simple Past *do* becomes *did*.

What is the question form? _____ you play football when you were a child?
What is the negative form? When I was a child I _____ football.
What are the short answers? Yes, _____ No, _____

[B] *To list* is a regular verb.

Look at the text below. Identify the
Simple Past affirmative of *to list*.
There are three other verbs in the text
which follow the same or a very similar
pattern.
Find them.
Can you see a rule?

[C] Does this rule apply to all verbs?
Look again at the text.
List the verbs which are in the Simple
Past which do not fit the rule.

Look at line 9. What is 'that'?
Look at line 10. What is 'her'?

Record name

BABY Tracy Nelson will take her place in the record books when she gets 140 Christian names at Barrow Hill, Chesterfield, today.

Bond winners

THE £100,000 Premium winner this week

Sunday Times 20.4.86.

What name did **you** get?

Trevor George loved football. He decided to name his new baby daughter after twenty world-famous football stars. So her birth certificate listed her name as: Jennifer Pele Jairzinho Rivelino Alberto Cesar Breitner Cryuff Greaves Charlton Best Moore Ball Keegan Banks Gray Francis Brooking Curtis Toshack Law George! Mrs George didn't like that and left home. The Registry Office allowed her to rename the child Jennifer Anne and a month later the couple got back together again.

From *And Finally* by Martyn Lewis.

Match the following words with their definitions:

to decide	an official document with details of a person's name, date and place of birth, etc.
to name	
birth certificate	to go back
to list	to make up your mind/to make a decision
to allow	Government Office to record births, marriages, deaths
Registry Office	
to return	to start a relationship again
to get back together	to permit
	to give a name to someone or something
	to write down a number of items in an order, e.g. alphabetically

2 In 1840 the French sailing ship the *Rosalie* sailed from France.
On board there was a full crew and a canary.

In September 1944 the *Rubicon*, a Cuban freighter, sailed from Havana. It carried a crew, a dog, and a full cargo.

Listen. What happened?

a sail   a sailor   a canary   a captain's log-book   a lifeboat   a life-jacket

Listen again.

Are these True or False?

a The *Rosalie* sailed for the Caribbean.
b When the boat was found
 – the sails were cut, torn into pieces.
 – the canary was dead.
c When the *Rubicon* was found
 – the log-book was not on the boat.
 – only the dog was on board.
 – the lifeboats were not on the boat.

3 Pairs

You were both on one of the ships. Decide which one. Imagine what happened. Both of you make notes. Your story must end '... and then everything went black.'

Change partners.

A: Use your story. Answer B's questions.
B: Ask questions to find out what happened on A's ship. Use the Simple Past tense. Ask as many questions as you can.

Now A ask B about his/her story.

Useful Language

What was the first thing you noticed?
What did you think it was?
Then what happened?
How did you feel?
Did you see/hear anything?

4 Class

How many possible solutions to the two mysteries can you think of? List them.

Language

Simple Past

Form

Affirmative: Regular – Subject + verb + ed *We talked about football.*
Irregular – Subject + past verb *I went there last year.*

Negative: Regular ⎤
Irregular ⎦ – Subject + did not (didn't) + verb *I didn't go.*

Interrogative: Regular ⎤
Irregular ⎦ – did + subject + verb *Did she go?*
When did she arrive?

Use

1 To talk about things that happened in the past when the time period is finished, e.g. *yesterday*
2 To tell stories

We use the Simple Past a great deal with the adverbials on page 66.
We also use it with *ago: I saw her two weeks ago.*
He left three days ago.

Some/any/every compounds

Complete this chart.

Mark the stress on each word, e.g. nobody. Use a dictionary.

	PERSON	OBJECT	PLACE
no	nobody	_____	_____
any	anybody	anything	_____
some	_____	_____	somewhere
every	_____	_____	_____

Vocabulary

Look through this unit (pages 70–73) and list ten words you want to learn. Choose the words which interest you; the ones which are useful to you. Check the meaning in a dictionary. Write one sentence with each word.

Developments 13

Read this text once quickly. Don't worry about the words you don't know.

Which of the solutions in the article did your class think of? (see No. 4 page 71)

Read it a second time and try to answer the questions below.

The mystery of the disappearing ships.

THE MYSTERIES of the *Rosalie* and the *Rubicon* are still mysteries today. Nobody knows what happened to their crews. Several other cases are recorded, one of the most famous being the *Marie Celeste*. But many other ships disappeared completely: nothing was left – no survivors, no wreckage. They just disappeared. The American warship the *USS Pickering* was the first recorded case: it disappeared in 1800 with 90 people on board.

In 1931 an aircraft disappeared. It was the first of many. One of the most famous cases was the disappearance of five American military aircraft. They radioed for help on December 5th 1945. A rescue aircraft left immediatly but not one of the six planes returned to base. The search was intensive but nothing... no bodies, no wreckage, no oil... was found. A count made in 1977, of lost crews, ships and planes noted a total of 143 disappearances. A very great number of these occurred in the 1960's and 1970's.

The possible solutions to these mysteries are difficult to believe. One suggested solution is illness. If it was an illness, then it killed everybody. Did someone throw all the bodies overboard? Did that person then jump overboard? But perhaps it was a mental illness and everybody on board went mad and jumped overboard! Pirates are another possibility: they exist today just as they did in the 18th and 19th centuries. Today they can take small speedboats, repaint them and use them for smuggling. But pirates also want cargoes, and on the *Rubicon* and other ships the cargoes were complete.

Storms, heavy seas, high winds and waterspouts can all destroy ships and planes, but usually something is found later... some wreckage, bits of wood, oil, lifejackets, etc.

Some people believe that there is a 'hole' in our space/time dimension and that ships and planes pass through the hole to another world in a different time and space. Others believe that extra-terrestrials take the ships, crews and planes, in a form of kidnapping – 'spacenapping'.

All these mysteries happened in or near the so-called Bermuda Triangle. But such events also occur at the opposite side of the world, not far from Japan, in an area called Devil's Sea.

There are many other strange events associated with these two areas. When will we know the answer?

1 *(to) disappear* is a verb. Find the noun in the passage.

2 A *survivor* is:
someone who dies
someone who calls for help
someone who lives after a difficult time

3 *Wreckage* is:
bits and pieces from a boat or plane
a type of boat
old clothes

4 *on board* = on the ship. Find the word for 'out of the ship'.

5 *(to) rescue, (to) destroy, (to) find* are all verbs used in the passage. What is the past tense of each?

6 *Smuggling* is a crime. It means taking things illegally into a country. There is another crime in the passage. Find it. What does it usually mean? What does it mean here?

7 Find the word which means 'people from another world'.

8 Find another word for 'to happen'.

Unit 14

1 [A] Listen to the story. Put the pictures into the correct order.

[B] Listen again. Now put the story into the correct order.

1 On 11 October 1932 Bonnie and Clyde arrived in the town of Sherman, Texas.
2 Bonnie stayed in the car with a shotgun and watched the street.
3 He ordered some Bologna sausage and cheese and waited while the storekeeper cut them.
4 It was early afternoon and the streets were empty.
5 Clyde walked into the store.
6 The storekeeper picked up a meat knife. Clyde shot him and took 28 dollars.
7 Finally after twelve murders and two years on the run the police ambushed Bonnie and Clyde. A group of policemen waited by the highway for two days. When Bonnie and Clyde drove past the police 'filled them full of bullets'.
8 Clyde dashed out of the store. Bonnie started the car. Bonnie and Clyde roared off in a cloud of dust.
9 When the storekeeper handed him the sausage and cheese Clyde pulled out a pistol and demanded money.
10 Slowly, they parked their Ford V8 outside the general store.

14

2 Look at the transcript on page 74. Underline all the past tense regular (*-ed*) verbs.

Listen to the story and read the transcript. Place each regular verb in the correct column. Practise saying the verbs to your partner.

Pronunciation

The *-ed* has three possible pronunciations: [t], [d], [id].
For example:
walked [t]
pulled [d]
waited [id]

Make three columns like this:

[t]	[d]	[id]
	travelled	

3 Groups

Imagine a bank robbery. Decide who plays what part: robbers, customers, clerks, manager.

Who says what?
'Get your hands up.'
'Lie down.'
'I can't, I've no key.'
'Oh no, ... help, it's a ...'

'Here, here you are.'
'Don't move.'
'It won't open.'
'Look out. They're coming.'

Add your own phrases/sentences. You don't have to use all of the above ones.
Act out your play.

Handicapped burglar ticked off by judge.

At York Crown Court a one-legged burglar with a glass eye and a deformed hand was sentenced to ninety days community service.

The judge told Philip McCutcheon: "You're a rotten burglar. Whoever heard of a burglar with one leg, something wrong with his hand, and a glass eye. Don't you think it's time you gave up crime?"

Language

Spelling: Simple Past tense

Regular verbs

[A] Most do this:
  start – start*ed*
  walk – walk*ed*
  play – play*ed*
  wait – wait*ed*
  demand – demand*ed*

  Rule: For most verbs take the base of the _____ and _____

[B] Some do this:
  live – live*d*
  decide – decide*d*
  love – love*d*

  Rule: For verbs which end in _____ add _____

[C] Some do this:
  stud*y* stud*ied*
  worr*y* worr*ied*
  empt*y* empt*ied*

  Rule: For verbs which end in consonant + *y* change the _____ into _____ and _____ *ed*

[D] Some do this:
  sto*p* – sto*pp*e*d*
  trave*l* – trave*ll*e*d*
  ro*b* – ro*bb*e*d*

  Rule: For verbs which end consonant + vowel + consonant with stress on the last syllable double the last _____ and add _____

Irregular verbs

These do not end in *-ed*. Each verb has its own rule.
Match the present and past forms of these verbs:

Present	Past
go	came
buy	saw
see	bought
come	went

Form the past tense of these verbs: get, have, leave, make, put, run, choose.

Vocabulary

Check you understand these verbs. Use a dictionary. Write one sentence with each verb.

to stay, to watch, to order, to wait, to pick up something, to hand something to someone, to shoot, to take, to demand something

76

Developments

Headlines These are all short articles from *The Guardian* newspaper. Match each headline to an article.

SOUTH Africa's Hugo Vanpe, yesterday established a world marathon hairdressing record when he put down his scissors after 15 days of non-stop styling. — Reuter.

Guardian 25.6.84. [a]

BRITAIN and South Korea yesterday signed an agreement to provide direct air links between the two countries. — Reuter.

Guardian 6.3.84. [b]

BRITAIN boosted its champagne consumption by almost 50 per cent in the first six months of the year, downing seven million bottles to overtake the US as the biggest export market for bubbly.

Guardian 19.8.85. [c]

A YOUTH from the French island of Guadeloupe committed suicide at his parents' home near Paris after they refused to pay for plastic surgery he hoped would make him look like his hero, the American singer Michael Jackson, police reported. — AP.

Guardian 5.7.84. [d]

FRANCE is ending reverse charge telephone calls from today because the service, in use for 50 years, has run up a deficit of 100 million francs (£8.4 million). — Reuter.

Guardian 2.9.85. [e]

ANATOLY Karpov and Gary Kasparov meet in Moscow's Tchaikovsky concert hall today in a ceremony marking the resumption of their world chess title combat. Their previous contest was abandoned inconclusively after 48 games. Under new rules the two men play a maximum 24 games, with Karpov retaining his title if they finish with 12 points each. — Reuter.

Guardian 2.9.85. [h]

A BRAZILIAN housemaid gave birth to her tenth set of twins in Rio on Tuesday. Mrs Maria Goncalves Moreira, aged 42, herself a twin, says that double births run in the family — her mother also produced 10 sets of twins. — AP.

Guardian 5.7.84. [f]

VENICE in an effort to check the city's growing pigeon menace is feeding the birds contraceptive food. The mayor said pigeons were dirtying and damaging Venice's historic buildings and monuments. — AP.

Guardian 3.7.84. [g]

FORTUNE-telling has become a major social disease in the Soviet Union and is ruining many lives, the trade union paper Trud says. — Reuter.

Guardian 19.8.85. [i]

Bubbly Britain   **Air deal**   **Square one**

Unfortunate   **War on pigeons**

Hairy record   **Twins again**   **Fatal choice**

Rung off

Unit 15

1 Listen to the tape.
What do these noises sound like?

2 Listen again to the tape. The sounds tell a story.
What is the story? Make notes. Do not write full sentences.

Pairs
Try to tell each other the story from your notes.
Listen to the story on the tape. Is it similar to yours or very different?

3 Listen to the tape again. Tick √ which of these 'linking' expressions you hear:
a moment later
however
after
then
suddenly
on the other hand
so

4 Pairs
What happened next? Finish the story.

5 Pairs
Now listen to the sounds of another story. Makes notes. Tell the story.

Egg cracked in time for dinner

Twelve-year-old James Showers from East Sussex hatched the egg of a wild duck by keeping it in his armpit for three weeks. He said 'I found it abandoned under a hedge during the school holidays.' It eventually hatched at dinner time at his boarding school at Oxford. Too late to change the menu, though!

Adapted from *And Finally* by Martyn Lewis.

Language

15

Linkers

'Linkers' are the words and phrases which join language together.
They help us organize what we want to say; help us to show the relationship between two 'ideas'.

Examples:

and
joins two main pieces of information.
He put his key in the lock and opened the door.

then
shows that the second piece of information follows the first.
He took out a glass, then he poured a drink.

a moment later
shows the time between the first and second events.
A moment later he switched on the television.

suddenly
introduces something unexpected/important.
Suddenly a voice said . . .

Verb +*like*

Look at picture 1. What is this black stuff? Are you sure?
We don't know exactly what it is. So we say: *It looks like oil.*

We can use this pattern with 'to sound' and some other verbs.
Complete the caption to each picture.
Use these verbs: sound, taste, smell, look, feel.
And think of a good ending.

1 It _looks_ like _oil._

3 It ____ like ____

5 It ____ like ____

2 It ____ like ____

4 It ____ like ____

6 It ____ like ____

Vocabulary

Make a list of all the adjectives you can find in the *Developments* section of this unit. Check meaning. What 'things' can you use each adjective to describe?
For example: *ugly* – faces/places/people/buildings/towns.

Developments

[A] Jane wrote a postcard on each of these dates. Which is the correct date for each postcard?

20.6.84   4.7.84   7.7.84   30.6.84

Jane's America

Dear Auntie,
The last stop - all good things come to an end. Landed in thick fog in San Francisco but it's a fantastic place - you'd love it. There are so many different cultures and there's such a lot happening here! I can't believe I'll be back home in a few days. Looking forward to seeing you.
Love Jane

Dear Rob,
Drove to Durango, stayed overnight, then on to Mesa Verde - very old Indian cave villages - fascinating. Of course we went to the Grand Canyon - every tourist has to! It's quite enormous and very beautiful. Now in Las Vegas which is hot, ugly and very unpleasant. Hope all is well with you.
Love Jane xxx

Dear Marina,
Left London late - long tiring flight. Dallas is HOT!!! 40°. Everything is very big and ultra modern. Lots of old friends at the exhibition so we are all having fun. It's really true - Texan men wear enormous hats and cowboy clothes.
Love Jane xxx

Dear Rick and Vicky,
Flew to Denver on Tuesday and hired a car. Lovely cool air after Dallas!! and amazing scenery. Stayed with friends in Boulder for three days. Now in Ouray - an old mining town in the mountains - looks like the towns you see in cowboy films. Hope you are well. Lots of love to Charlie.
Jane xxx

15

[B] Jane visited nine places. Mark her route on your map. Mark how she travelled (by bus, train, etc.)

[C] These pictures represent some of the places that Jane visited. Listen to the tape and name the places.
Listen again. What did Jane do in each of these places?

1 _____

2 _____
Stayed with friends.

3 _____

4 *Mesa Verde*

5 _____
Watched a thunder storm.

6 _____

81

Unit 16

16

1 Look at the picture.

Imagine you were the photographer. What were the people doing at the moment you took the photograph?

2 Listen.

What was happening that night?
What happened to the necklace?

Listen again. Choose the correct answers:

a The diamonds were
- in a cupboard.
- on Lady Felicity's neck.
- on a table.
- in the bedroom.

b A blackout is
- when day changes to night.
- when you turn the lights off.
- when the lights go off.

c The blackout lasted for
- 2–3 seconds.
- exactly 3 minutes.
- 2–3 minutes.

d The 'finger of suspicion' points at
- one of the guests.
- one of the guests or servants.
- one of the servants.
- Inspector Trouvé.

16

3 Imagine you are a detective. Prepare a list of questions to ask the guests. For example:
name?
where/you/when/lights/go/out?
what/you/do?
you/see/anyone?

4 Study your role card carefully.
Do not show it to anyone.
Do not discuss it with anyone.
Check you understand everything. Ask your teacher; use a dictionary.

You are two people: 1 – a detective; 2 – a guest.
As the detective, you interview all the guests and make notes.
As the guest, you answer all the detective's questions.

Pairs
(i) A (detective) → interviews → B (guest)
(ii) B (detective) → interviews → A (guest)
Repeat steps (i) and (ii) with all the other students. Do *not* speak about your ideas.

5 Study your notes. Look for clues.

6 Class

Who do you think stole the necklace?
Why?

Listen. The inspector gives the answer. Were you right?

Language 16

Past Continuous

Form

Affirmative: Subject + was/were + verb + *ing* | *She was dancing.*

Negative: Subject + was not (wasn't)/were not (weren't) + verb + *ing* | *They weren't talking.*

Interrogative: Was/Were + subject + verb + *ing* | *Was it working? Where were you sitting?*

Use

1 To describe a scene, usually when you tell a story
The old man was walking slowly down the street.
The two boys were following him ...

2 To talk about something happening at a particular moment in the past
I was working at 10 o'clock last night.

3 To talk about an action in progress, interrupted by another action
He was dancing when the lights went out.

Vocabulary

Check you understand these words. Use a dictionary.
Listen to the tape again. Tick √ the words when you hear them.
Write sentences for each word.

Nouns: guests, a theft, a party, details

Adjectives: simple, luxurious

Verbs: wear, take off, interview, meet, catch

Developments

[A]

The accident described here happened on the ninth of March 1984. The article appeared in *The Guardian* newspaper on the following day. Complete the text. Use the list of verbs below to fill in the blanks. Check the verb is in the correct form.
Use each once:
have, fall, save, look, escape, think, happen, crash

Mrs. Janet Hill (right) _____ with a cut finger yesterday when her Ford Escort car _____ through a safety barrier in a multi-storey car-park and _____ 25 feet on to the roof of Lloyds Bank (below) in Dawlish, Devon. Mrs. Hill, aged 64, said "Something _____ to the engine of my car. It's an automatic. It just seemed to career forward and keep going. My seat belt _____ me." Lloyds manager, Mr. Ken Treneman, aged 55, _____ the bank was being raided. "I could hear this fantastic noise above me and flattened myself against the office wall, expecting the worst. I _____ up and couldn't believe my eyes. There was this red Escort against my office skylight, and the glass hadn't even broken." Mrs. Hill, of Kingsdown Crescent, Dawlish, _____ a checkupp in hospital and was sent home. The car, which will be winched off the roof today, is a write-off.

Glossary

a safety barrier – a very strong fence or wall, e.g. in the middle of a motorway
a multi-storey car park – a car park with two or more floors
to career forward – to go forward quickly, suddenly out of control
raided (to raid) – to attack and steal money
skylight – a window in the roof
a check-up – a routine medical examination
winched (to winch) – to lift with machinery
a write-off – something which cannot be repaired; too badly damaged

a *I couldn't believe my eyes* means 'I didn't believe what I saw'. We can also use this expression for what we hear.
So we can say: I _____ meaning, 'I didn't _____

b *and the glass hadn't even broken*
  (i)   Was the skylight broken?
  (ii) Was the speaker surprised?
  (iii) Which word tells you the answer to (ii)?

Here are two more examples:
Mrs Hill wasn't even hurt.
The car didn't even turn over.

c What is the printing mistake in the original newspaper article?

86

[B]

This is the view from the car park

You are Ms Johnson from Dawlish.
You were in the car park, getting into your car when the accident happened.
What did you see?
What did you think?
What did you do?

A little later you received the following letter from Mrs Hill's insurance company.

The Sun National Insurance Group Ltd   Sun National House
22–24 Okehampton Road
London EC1

Roseland Cottage
10 High Street
Dawlish   10 April 1984

Dear Ms Johnson,

We understand that you witnessed an accident on 9th March 1984 in the Dawlish multi-storey car park. The accident involved a Ford Escort car driven by Mrs Hill. We would be very grateful if you could please write a brief description, stating what you saw.

Thanking you in advance.

Yours sincerely,

J Peters

16

Complete the following letter. First put the words in each sentence in the correct order. Then put the sentences in the correct order. If you prefer, write your own story.

ran edge the looked and I to down

getting car when career was saw the I Escort, I into my forward

rather she looked do not she was I hurt think but upset

twenty feet car below was about roof on me a the and getting driver was the slowly out

crashed seemed to straight barrier the safety control and be through of out it

```
                                          Roseland Cottage
                                          10 High Street
                                          Dawlish


                                          10 April 1984


The Sun National Insurance Group Ltd
Sun National House
22-24 Okehampton Road
London EC1

Dear Mr Peters,

Thank you for your letter. I was in the car park

on the 9th March 1984. ─────────────────────────

_____

_____

_____

_____

_____


I hope this information is useful to you.

Yours sincerely,

    Barbara Johnson
    Barbara Johnson
```

Unit 17

1 Listen to the tape.

Three people saw picture A. They *disliked* the picture.
Three people saw picture B. They *liked* the picture.
Decide which people saw picture A and
which people saw picture B.

	Picture A	Picture B
1		
2		
3		
4		
5		
6		

Which speaker shows the strongest positive feelings?
What language do they use?
Which speaker shows the strongest negative feelings?
What language do they use?

The speakers saw the two animal pictures on
pages 134 and 136.
What are they? What do you think/feel about
them?

Pronunciation

Listen again.
What are the 'noises' which mean 'I dislike'/'I like'.
Practise them.

Practise the intonation of these phrases:
'I just can't stand those things.'
'I really don't like them.'
'Aren't they lovely.'
'I suppose they're OK.'

2 Pairs

Look at the pictures on page 90.
Which pictures do you like, dislike, loathe or
love?
Which pictures have you no feeling about?
Can you say why you like or dislike any of
these pictures?
Is it the style of the picture?
Is it the content of the picture?
Look back through the book. How do you
feel about other pictures?

17

3 Here are some things that people like or don't like doing.
Tick ✓ the ones you like doing.

Washing the dishes after a dinner party.
Curling up by the fire with a book on a cold wet day.
Driving a fast car or motor cycle on country roads in the early morning.
Standing on a mountain top in windy weather.
Going around the shops buying groceries.
Walking along the beach on a warm summer evening.
Travelling to work every morning on a crowded train.
Lying all day in the sun by a swimming pool.

Add two things to the list that you really like doing.
Add two things that you really can't stand doing.

Class

Find out about other people. Is there one (or more) things on the list that you *all* like doing or loathe doing?

4

RAT DATA

RAT CATCH
An Indonesian village chief thought of a clever tax system to fight a plague of rats. Couples must pay 10 rats to marry and 20 for a divorce.

The Guardian 20.7.85.

WAR ON RATS
President Suharto yesterday ordered the Indonesian armed forces to fight one of mankind's oldest enemies – voracious rats gobbling food supplies. The rodents this year have destroyed more than 55,000 acres of rice.

The Guardian 5.9.85.

RAT SPEAK
The rat race – the competition for jobs, salaries, houses, cars, etc.
To look like a rat's nest – very untidy, dirty, e.g. hair
To be ratty – to be bad tempered, a bit angry
To look like a drowned rat – to be very very wet, usually with your clothes on
To smell a rat – to think that something is wrong or suspicious

RAT FACTS
A female rat can have about 8 baby rats every three weeks.
Rats probably eat about 10% of the world's crops.
Total human population of Great Britain = 57 million.
Total rat population of Great Britain = 57 million.

RAT PHENOMENA
A rat king is a group of rats joined together by their tails. The term rat king first appeared in a dictionary written in 1557. Between 1654 and 1963 fifty-seven rat kings were found in Europe, most of them alive.

5 Groups

Think of an animal, any animal. Write a data sheet like the one above for your animal. Think of some idioms and some interesting facts.

Language

Likes and dislikes

[A] Look at these examples:
I loathe nuclear weapons.   *I loathe fighting.*
I love children.   *I love eating good food.*

When we describe what we like/dislike we can use two patterns:

Subject + verb + noun   Subject + verb + verb + ing

I | love / like / don't like / loathe | war / rain / spiders / swimming / riding / dancing

[B] We also use idioms to express likes and dislikes.

1 Subject + can't stand + noun / verb + ing   *He can't stand rats.* *He can't stand driving.*

2 Subject + be + fond / not fond + of + noun / verb+ing   *She's fond of cats.* *She's fond of walking.*

3 Subject + do / does + not mind + noun / verb+ing   *I don't mind spiders.* *I don't mind touching snakes.*

[C]
strongest like → love / like / be fond of / not mind / not be fond of / not like / loathe/can't stand ← strongest dislike

I think it's/they're
I suppose it's/she's
I don't think he's/they're
I think they're/she's

fantastic/great/marvellous/
nice/good/interesting
all right/not bad
very good/interesting
horrible/terrible/awful

Vocabulary

Some words look the same in different languages:
to use (English) *usare* (Italian) *user* (French).
The meaning is sometimes different, sometimes similar, sometimes the same. Look through this unit and make a list of all the words which look similar to a word in your language. Check the meaning carefully. Write example sentences for the English words.

Developments

This story is also on tape. Use the material in any way you like. You can read, or listen, or read and listen simultaneously. Choose which is best for *you*.

KING RAT

Glossary

throat – The tube for air, food, etc. between the mouth and the body
disease – illness
(to) escape – to get away
(to) complain – to say that something is wrong; to protest
The Black Death – Bubonic Plague, a disease which kills
The plague – see The Black Death
anthrax – a disease
(to) feel sorry for someone – to be unhappy about someone's state or condition, e.g. you feel sorry for someone who is sick, has a lot of problems, etc.
charms – nice things; good qualities
champion – winner of competitions, e.g. World Champion
sweetcorn – a vegetable; maize
boarding house – a small hotel
a cage – a house/container for animals and birds
to exhibit – to show in an exhibition
a show – a type of exhibition
a founder member – original member
extinct – not in the world any more, e.g. dinosaurs
miserable – very unhappy
hamster, ferret, gerbil – different types of small furry animals

Nobody likes rats. Everyone thinks they are dirty, carry diseases, bite people's throats and steal eggs from chickens. If you call someone a 'rat' they know you don't like them. Someone in a 'ratty mood' is not much fun and 'the rat race' is something we all try to escape from. Few people protest or complain when rats are used in laboratory experiments. Many people think rats were responsible for the Black Death which killed half the population of England in the Middle Ages.

But Sarah Handley shares her house with 40 rats and she doesn't think rats started the plague. She says "Some scientists think the plague was anthrax (a virus) and was carried by the wind. The plague spread very quickly; rats cannot travel so far or so fast." Sarah is trying to change people's opinions of rats. She says rats do not jump at throats... "If cornered a rat will go for the area of most daylight and so they jump up and over the shoulder." Sarah feels sorry for all of us who do not know the 'charms' of rats.

King of the rats in the Handley household is Solo. He is a show champion, and the family pet. While the other rats sleep in an empty bedroom, Solo sleeps with Sarah and her husband William, in his own cage in their bedroom. He gets up and breakfasts with them and in the evening sits at the kitchen table while Sarah cooks dinner. He helps himself to what he wants from their plates. He likes rice, sweetcorn and peas; he carefully removes the skin from the peas and he only eats the sweet insides. Later he has a few nuts and raisins, usually taking them from Sarah's lips in a delicate rat kiss. Uninvited he puts his long pointed nose into Sarah's wine glass, though his favourite drink is coke.

The Handleys take Solo with them when they go on holiday in the UK. In a big hotel they don't tell anybody. Nobody really notices a small cage. Last year they went to a small hotel so they asked for permission first. The hotel answered that he was welcome but wasn't allowed to eat in the dining-room.

Sarah stole her first rat from her brother. He kept rats as food for his snakes. Her family always had lots of animals but only Sarah liked rats. She first kept them as pets, then she started to exhibit them at shows. In 1976 she became a founder member of the National Fancy Rat Society.

There are several colours and types of rats. Sarah saved the Cinnamon Pearl (Solo is a fine example) when it nearly went extinct. Now there are several hundred all descended from the original pair.

All her rats have lovely characters except for Orlando who lives alone because he is so unfriendly. "He was always miserable," says Sarah. "I bought him because I felt sorry for him."

Although Solo is everybody's favourite, the others come down to play in the living room every day. "They're perfect pets," says Sarah "People are so silly about them. They come up to me at shops and say 'Ooh what is it? Is it a hamster? or a ferret? or a gerbil? Then you say 'No, it's a rat' and they fall backwards. People are really ignorant about rats."

Adapted from *King Rat*, J. Wheatley, *You* magazine.

Unit 18

1

This gesture means 'A-okay' in many parts of the world but in many places it is a very rude gesture.

On his first trip to Naples, a well-meaning American tourist thanks his waiter for a good meal well-served by making the "A-Okay" gesture with his thumb and forefinger. The waiter pales and heads for the manager. They seriously discuss calling the police and having the hapless tourist arrested for obscene and offensive public behaviour.

What happened?

Psychology Today, May 1984

Glossary

well-meaning – wanting to be polite
pales (to pale) – goes white
heads for (to head for) – goes to
hapless – unlucky

Gesture is part of language.

Watch the people around you. Do they scratch, play with their hair, or touch their faces when they talk? Do you? How would you show 'I'm hungry' to someone who doesn't speak your language? What do people do with their arms an hands when they are excited?

Some gestures have very strong meanings and they are understood by most of the people in an area or group. Speakers of different languages or people from different areas, or groups, may use the same gesture to mean different things.

This gesture in Russia means 'friendship'... in the United States it means 'I am the winner'.

18

2 Groups

These gestures are widely understood in Britain.

1 'Mind your own business' or 'It's a secret'.
2 Hoping for good luck.
3 This gesture is often used by children. It is a mockery or insult.
4 'Victory' or 'peace'.
5 'Good', 'fine' or 'OK'.

Groups
Tell each other:
if the gestures mean the same in your country.
if they mean something different.
if they don't mean anything at all.

3 [A] These next gestures are quite rare in Britain. Do they mean anything where you live? How often are they used? Which groups of people use them?

[B] Can you think of gestures from your country to say:
1 'I'm not interested'?
2 'There isn't any' or 'There aren't any'?
3 'Yes'?
4 'That's good'?

[C] Groups
Think of as many different gestures as you can from as many countries/areas as possible. How often is each gesture used?

Class
Put together the information from each group.

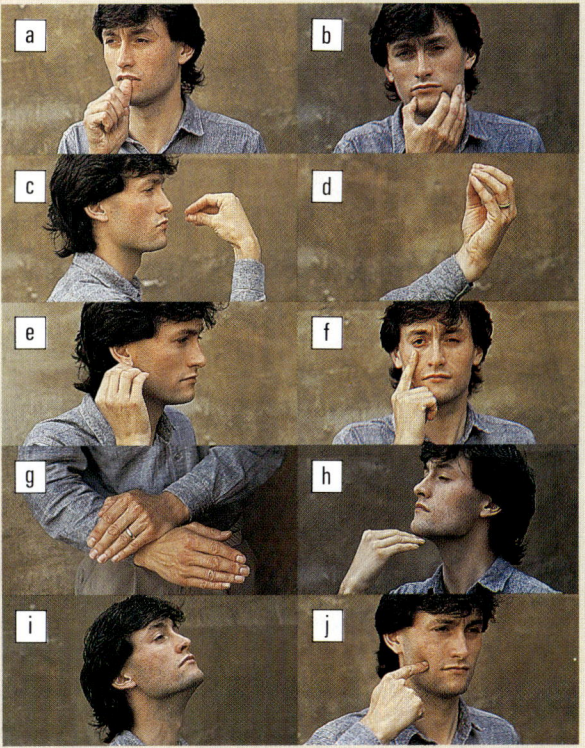

[D] Groups
Invent gestures to mean:
1 'I'm thirsty.'
2 'It's very expensive.'
3 'Not this one, that one.'
4 'I don't understand.'
5 'I don't know.'

Compare yours with other groups' gestures.

Useful Language

That means ... in ...
We don't use that.
It's a terrible insult.
We always do this.
It can sometimes mean ...
They often use that in ...

95

18

4 Being rude in English depends on two things:
1 What you say
2 How you say it

It is very easy to be rude by mistake, if you speak in an abrupt tone and do not say *please* or *thank you*.

When you want to be really rude you can use the expressions on the right. You can also use these expressions to be jokingly rude to a friend. Remember that these expressions change from one English-speaking country to another and they also change with 'fashions' in language.

Describing someone

Adjectives
bloody
silly
damn
crazy
stupid
idiotic

Calling someone names

Nouns
fool
idiot
moron
lunatic

Telling someone to go away

Verbs
get lost
push off
get knotted

Pronunciation

Listen.
On the tape some people are really angry/upset.
　　　　　 some people are joking with friends.

Decide which are seriously rude.
　　　　which are jokingly rude.

Listen again. Tick ✓ which of the above expressions are used.

5

Pairs

Where are these people?
How do they feel?

Make notes on the conversation just before the gesture.
Do you think this gesture is the end of the conversation?
Write notes on anything they say afterwards.
Act out your dialogue.

Useful Language

I was just ... when you ...
You walked out right in front of me ...
Damn fool ... why don't you look where you're going!
Silly idiot!
That was a bloody silly thing to do.
What do you think you're doing, you fool!
Ah, get lost!

Language

18

Adverbs of frequency	**Use** To say 'how often' something happens.

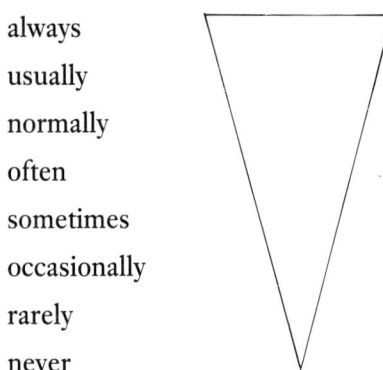

always
usually
normally
often
sometimes
occasionally
rarely
never

Word order	The most common order is: Person + (auxiliary) + adverb + verb ... *I don't often go out.* *She sometimes stays here.* *He can never get it right.*
Vocabulary	Look through this unit and make a list of the words which occur frequently. Check the meaning carefully. Write example sentences.

Developments

Describing people

[A]

(i) Look at these pictures.
What can you say about each woman?

(ii) Now listen to the tape. Two people are talking about Betty Sharp. Which is the photograph of Betty?

(iii) Listen again. There are seven pieces of information about Betty. List them.

> She's got short hair.
> It's _____   _____
> She _____   _____
> _____

[B] Someone called Eddie is described in this letter.

(i) Read it and underline the six pieces of information about him.

> Dear Paula,
> I'm glad you like your new life. Just don't work too hard, and remember to write. I'll try and send you the gossip from here...... and talking of gossip...... guess who was round here last night. Eddie Shaw! You probably won't remember the name, let me describe him...... well he works in the office downstairs – always drives a dirty old Mini...... He's good looking though. He's got glasses and he smokes...... but he is very funny, really makes me laugh. And he...... well we're going out on Saturday so I'll tell you more in my next letter.
> The office isn't the same without you......

(ii) Look again at the description of Eddie.

Look at the grammar.
How many examples of the *has/have got* are there?
How many examples of the Simple Present?
How many examples of *to be* + adjective?
We use these constructions to describe people.

[C] Think of someone you know/someone in the room.

Think about:
– the colour of their hair/eyes.   – their style of dress.
– the length of their hair.   – their habits.
– their height.

Use the grammatical forms in (ii) above and write 5–8 sentences describing the person.

Unit 19

1 Expeditions

GANGES WALK

Dennison Berwick's sandals were mended 50 times during his seven-month walk along the River Ganges – 1,557 miles from delta to source. This walk provided his mother, Mrs Margaret Berwick, Vice-Chairman of our UK Committee, with a "golden opportunity" to raise funds on behalf of SCF and a special committee of supporters in West Yorkshire worked to attract sponsors.

Save The Children Magazine
December 1984

On her bike

What makes a 45-year-old mother of three cycle 5,000 miles across India and top it by riding through dacoit country, and over a 10,000 foot Himalayan pass? Bettina Selby talks to Guardian Women.

Guardian 25.6.85.

Solo sailor Simon home

British yachtsman Simon Wall, 24, is expected back in Plymouth tomorrow to become the youngest solo sailor to complete a two-way Trans-Atlantic voyage.

Simon, from Oadby, Leicester, left Plymouth in the 30ft sloop Spirit of Leicester on May 1 and reached Newport, Rhode Island, in six weeks.

Sunday Express 14.7.85.

Globe-trotters

RUNNERS Henry Weston, 22, and Robin Cross, 23, set off from London yesterday on a 15,500-mile round-the-world jog, with a friend taking supplies on a push-bike.

Daily Mirror 4.4.84.

Read the above articles. Complete the information.

	Transport	Route
D. Berwick	_____	_____
Weston + Cross	_____	_____
B. Selby	bicycle	across India
S. Wall	_____	_____

2 Pairs

Think about Bettina Selby's trip. What things did she take?
Look at this list of items. Decide which items she had to take and which she didn't have to take.

Had to take	*Didn't have to take*
_____	_____
_____	_____
_____	_____
_____	_____
_____	_____
_____	_____
_____	_____
_____	_____
_____	_____
_____	_____
_____	_____

travel documents
maps
bicycle puncture kit
plastic rain-coat/poncho
2 pairs of comfortable shoes
bicycle tool kit
sunglasses
camera
small first aid kit
face cleaning creams
binoculars
1 pair of trousers
1 skirt
a diary
2 shirts
2 T-shirts
small personal stereo (Sony Walkman)
1 spare wheel
2 sets of underwear
2 pairs of socks
shampoo
a book for reading
a few rings
earring
1 hat
paper tissues
tooth brush and tooth paste
face cloth
a small portable typewriter
1 jumper
pen and paper
4 or 5 personal family photos
mosquito net
1 torch
2 water bottles
sleeping bag

You are planning a trip round India by bicycle.
Do you want to add anything to the 'have to' list?
Which things on the 'don't have to' list will you take with you?

3 Groups

What is the difference between an expedition and a tourist trip?
Why do people go on expeditions?

Plan an expedition for your group.
Look at the world map. Decide where you will go and why.
What transport will you use?
How will you live?
What will you need to take with you?
What preparations will you have to make?
Prepare: notes, lists, plans.

Useful Language

Why don't we choose . . . ?
We don't really need that.
Do we have to?
Why do we need that?
What will we need to get ready?

4 What is the cartoon about?

Groups

You are administrators in the Republic of Bognor. Your job is to make life difficult for foreign visitors to the country. You must introduce a system of exit visas – that is permission to leave the country. Decide what each foreign visitor has to do and who they must see before they can leave the country.

Think about:

Passports
Health certificates
Bills/taxes
Are they wanted by the police?
Do they have pets/documents/ vaccinations?
What different departments will they have to visit? What hours are those departments open?
How many/what pieces of paper will they need? Will they need signatures/stamps?

Useful Language

How difficult can we make this?
Let's think of the documents they need.
Who do they have to see?
So they have to . . . , then . . . , and then . . .
They have to go to . . . to get . . . .
They can go to the . . . to . . . .

5 Class

Each group elects a spokesperson. S/he explains their scheme to the class. Which scheme is the most complex? The most bureaucratic?

In February 1982 the British government published a report. They wanted to save millions of pounds by reducing the number of government forms. They called a press conference and handed out an information pack which explained the report. The information pack was 200 pages long, weighing a kilo, and took many hours to read.

And Finally, Martyn Lewis

Language

to need

Form

to need something
to need to do something

Affirmative: I need a new passport.
She needs to leave the country urgently.

Negative: I do not (don't) need a visa.
He does not (doesn't) need to phone the Embassy.

Interrogative: Do you need a new passport?
Do I need to leave?
When does he need to go?

Use

To express necessity

do not need = not necessary

to have to

Form

to have to do something

Affirmative: He has to get a new visa.

Negative: I do not (don't) have to give you my name.

Interrogative: Does she have to wait?
Why does she have to wait?

Use

1 To express obligation *You have to pay.*
2 To express necessity *I have to go home; my father is ill.*

Note: We often use 'have got to do something' in spoken British English:
I have (I've) got to go.   Have they got to have a visa?

Pronunciation

have to be is pronounced [hæv tə bi]
Compare this with *to have* [tə hæv]
Practise *have* [hæv] and *have to* [hæv tə]

19

Necessity

Affirmative	Negative
necessary	not necessary
must do	—
have to do	don't have to do
need to do	don't need to do

Examples:
I must get a visa.
I have to get a visa.
I need to get a visa.
I don't have to get two copies.
I don't need to get two copies.

Compare **a** and **b**.

a I don't | have / need | to leave.   **b** I mustn't leave.

Decide if these sentences mean **a** or **b**.
1 I can stay if I want to.
2 Someone says I am not allowed to leave.
3 Something 'bad' will happen if I leave.
4 I can leave if I want to.

Clauses of purpose

(action) + *to* + intended result

She went home to make a phone call.
(action)   (intended result)

I'll go to the police station to register my address.
She went to her employer to ask for a copy of the contract.
She left to see her sick father.

Vocabulary

Look through this unit (page 99 – page 105) and list ten words you want to learn. Choose the words which interest you; the ones which are useful to you. Check the meaning in a dictionary. Write one sentence with each word.

Developments

[A] This is a children's song.
Underline all the clauses of purpose.

There was an old woman who swallowed a fly.
I don't know why she swallowed a fly.
Perhaps she'll die.

There was an old lady who swallowed a spider
That wriggled and tickled and tickled inside her.
She swallowed the spider <u>to catch the fly</u>
But I don't know why she swallowed the fly.
Perhaps she'll die.

There was an old woman who swallowed a bird
Now how absurd to swallow a bird.
She swallowed the bird <u>to catch the spider that
   wriggled and tickled and tickled inside her</u>.
She swallowed the spider <u>to catch the fly</u>, but I
   don't know why she swallowed the fly.
Perhaps she'll die.

There was an old woman who swallowed a cat.
Fancy that! She swallowed a cat.
She swallowed the cat <u>to catch the bird</u>, etc.

There was an old woman who swallowed a dog.
Oh what a hog to swallow a dog.
She swallowed the dog <u>to catch the cat</u>, etc.

There was an old woman who swallowed a cow,
I don't know how she swallowed a cow.
She swallowed the cow <u>to catch the dog</u>, etc.

There was an old woman who swallowed a horse.
She's dead of course.

[B] This story is also on tape. Use the material any way you like.
You can read
         listen
         listen and read simultaneously. Choose which is best for *you*.

Last time Eric Peters made a single-handed crossing of the Atlantic, he went by beer barrel, under sail. This time, he's planning to do it without the sail. Penny Chorlton reports.

Some people are perhaps happy to get their names in the Guinness Book of Records once: Eric Peters, lone transatlantic yachtsman, is trying to get his name in twice. Eric wants to beat his own astonishing test of self-endurance.

In 1982 Eric crossed the Atlantic – all 2,600 miles of it – NOT in an ocean-going yacht but in a beer barrel about two metres long. He took no engine, no anchor, no radio, no compass, and no sunglasses. He is now sorry that he didn't take a pair of sunglasses because his eyes, after 46 days at sea, got badly burned by the glare of the sun on the water.

Most of the people who knew him in Littlehampton, Sussex, thought he was nuts. He spent two years on the dole making his beer-barrel waterproof and unsinkable. Asked why he decided to do it, Eric explained: "Because I wanted to prove it was possible."

He asked the top 50 companies for help with his strange voyage; they all said 'no' – or ignored him. But someone gave him a small sail and someone else gave him a supply of peanuts and vitamins – and this was his basic diet along with some bran and olive oil. He in fact lived on half a litre of water a day. The recommended minimum is a litre and a half. This was recommended when he contacted Surgeon Commander Frank Golden, a survival expert at the Institute of Naval Medicine in Southampton.

"At first I thought Mr Peters was joking. Then when I realized he was serious I thought he was crackers," Commander Golden says, adding, "I tried to discourage him and to persuade him to try something safer like crossing the Thames."

Eric hitched a lift on a ship to the Canary Islands, and on Christmas Eve he set off. He took no books and his only luxury, a tape recorder to record his daily log, got wet and refused to work. Forty-six days later Commander Golden got a postcard from Guadeloupe in the French West Indies. Eric was safely across the Atlantic.

Eric was back in England this month because he wants to do it again, only this time from West to East and this time, without a sail.

So far he has had little success in trying to find sponsors for a rerun. But he is now making last-minute preparations for his epic, perhaps final voyage. There will be no tearful farewell; nothing more than a pint or two of beer at his send-off. A hero sets sail – without a sail.

(adapted from an article by Penny Chorlton in *The Guardian*)

Glossary

single-handed – alone; without help
beer-barrel – a large container for beer
anchor

compass
nuts – crazy; mad
on the dole – unemployed
waterproof – protected from water, e.g. a waterproof coat
unsinkable – cannot sink/fall to the bottom of the water
bran – outside skin of grain
less than –
recommended (to recommend) – to advise; suggest
minimum – the smallest quantity
survival – living in difficult conditions
expert – a specialist; a person with special knowledge
crackers – crazy; nuts; mad
to discourage – to tell/ask someone not to do something
to persuade – to tell/ask someone to do something
safer – less dangerous
hitched a lift (to hitch) – to ask for or get a free ride, usually in cars/lorries
Christmas Eve – the day before Christmas, i.e. 24th December
so far – until now

Unit 20

1 Pairs

A government runs a country. Every government is responsible for many different areas, for example, taxation, defence and housing.
Think of other areas and write them in the boxes.

Pronunciation

Underline the stress in each word in the chart, e.g. Gov<u>ern</u>ment
Compare your chart with others.

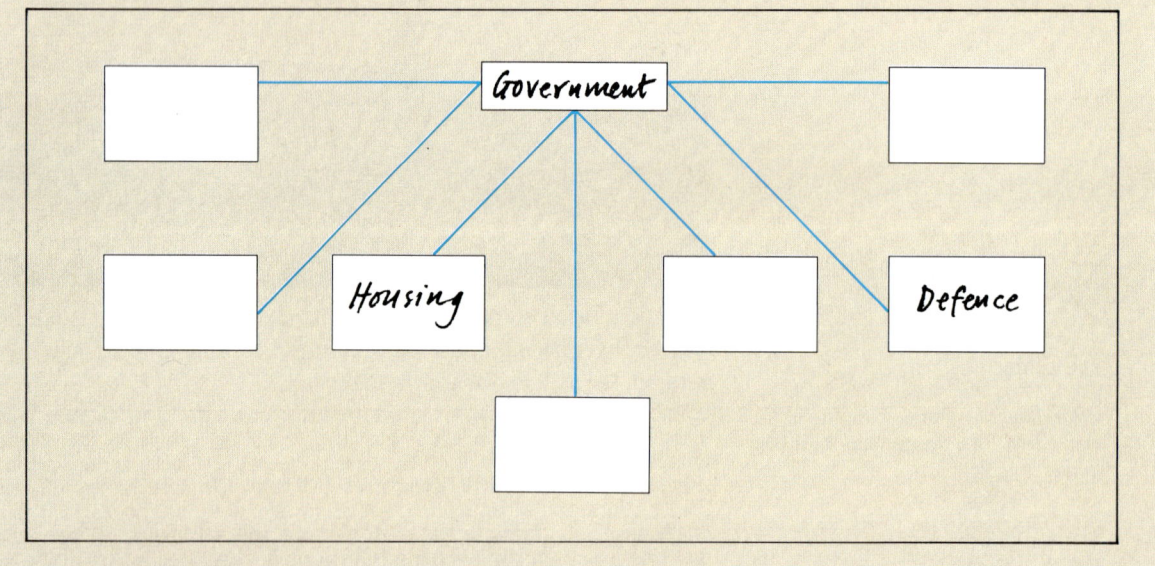

2 Listen.

The politician is making a speech before an election. Look at the list of possible intentions. Which things does the politician say their party is going to do?

Cut taxes
Put 10 million into education
Abolish military service
Reduce unemployment
Put 15 million dollars into housing
Build twenty new hospitals
Cut the army by 50%
Buy 50 new missiles for defence
Change the tax system
Increase state benefits, e.g. old age pensions
Reduce state benefits
Increase the school leaving age to 18
Introduce military service

3 Groups

You are members of a political party (for any real or imaginary country). Prepare a political manifesto.

Give your party a name.

Consider these areas:
taxation
social welfare
defence

What other areas can you think of?

Decide on the main points of your manifesto. Make a speech to the class and say what your party is going to do.

Useful Language

What'll we do about taxes?
So we'll do ..., ... and ...
The country needs ...
We'll have to increase/decrease ...
We're definitely going to ...
It's going to be difficult but ...
The public is going to ...

4 Pairs

[A] Listen to conversation 1.
What is going to happen next?
How many sentences can you make?
Compare yours with others in the class.

Listen to conversation 2.
What is going to happen next? Finish the story.
Tell your story to the class.

[B] Listen to this conversation.
What is she going to say next? Finish the conversation.

[C] Look at the situations in the pictures.
Fill in what s/he says.
Compare yours with others in the class.

Language

Going to: future

Form

Affirmative: Subject + { am / are / is / am } + going to + verb

We are going to build ten hospitals.

Negative: Subject + { are / is } + not (isn't, aren't) + going to + verb

He isn't going to do anything.

Interrogative: { am / are / is } + subject + going to + verb

Are you going to increase taxes?
What are you going to do?

Use

1 For future intentions which are already decided
  We're going to change the tax system.
2 A prediction of the future when the situation is clear
  The earth is going to get cooler. You're going to fall.

Future time adverbials

What is the date today? Put the correct date/s beside each expression.

tomorrow { morning _____ / afternoon _____ / evening _____ / night _____ }

The day after tomorrow. _____

next { week _____ / Monday/Tuesday _____ / month/year _____ }

The week after next. _____

Vocabulary

Look through this unit and make a list of all the words which look similar to a word in your language. Check the meaning carefully. Write sentences for the English words.

Developments   20

[A] Families

1

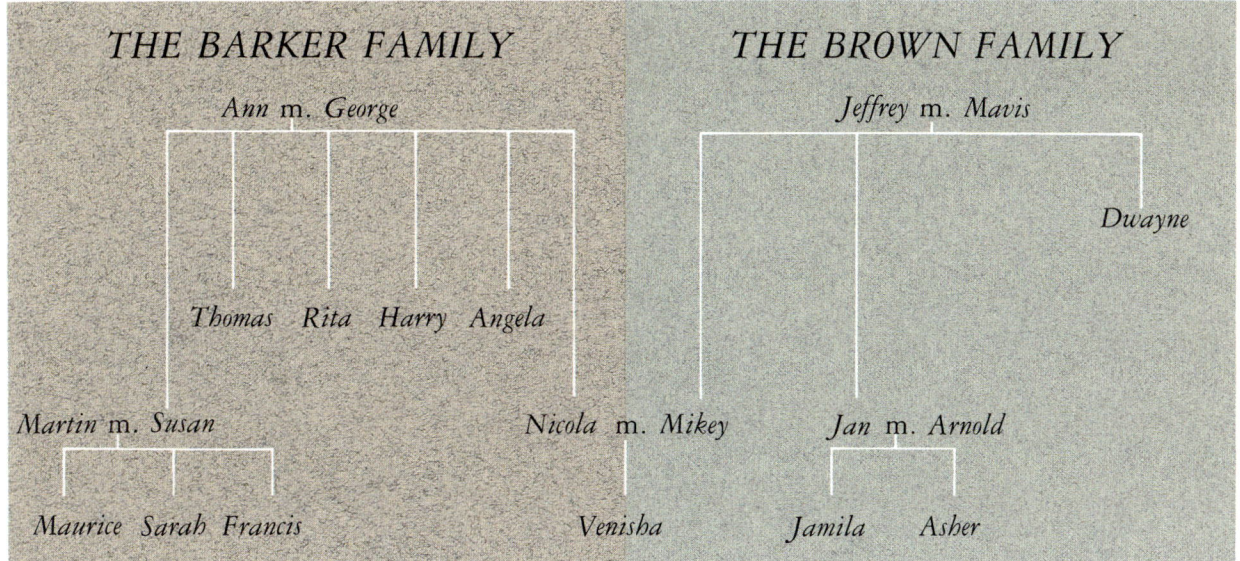

The Barker family are Mikey's in-laws (mother-in-law, father-in-law).
The _____ family are Nicola's in-laws (sister-in-law, brother-in-law, etc).

Venisha has 5 uncles. Name them.
She has 4 aunts. Name them.
She also has 5 cousins. Name them.
Nicola has 3 nieces and 2 nephews. Name them.

2 Some family relationships can be very complex. Look at this newspaper article and draw the family tree for this family.

Just read these articles.

Wedding in the family

HAPPY Barbara Hall was busy helping her dad get ready to marry again yesterday—to her mother-in-law.

Widower Harold Kidd, 61, is to marry the mother of Barbara's husband Peter tomorrow.

Barbara, from Paignton, Devon, said: "Now I'll be my dad's daughter AND daughter-in-law.

"My daughters are going to be bridesmaids—to their grandparents!"

Daily Mirror 7.9.84.

Much married

Windhoen (AP) – Rudolph Botha, aged 89, and his wife Joagamiena, 79, celebrated their 60th wedding anniversary this week – one of three wedding anniversaries they observe every year. They married each other three times – 1925, 1958 and 1974.

The Times 5.6.85.

Francois Aufret, from the island of Jersey took a long time to decide what kind of a life he wanted. After a 29-year engagement to his childhood sweetheart Agatha Kenchington, he finally named the day. He was 64. She was a sprightly 72. After the ceremony happy Agatha told reporters: "It's a big step, but I'm sure we'll never regret it."

And Finally, Martyn Lewis.

20

[B] These articles are all from *The Guardian* newspaper. Match the titles to the articles.

THREE hippos collapsed and died of shock when an elephant opened a valve with her trunk and sent piping hot water gushing into their pool at Karlsruhe Zoo, West Germany. The hippos were asleep in the pool when a 30-year-old female Indian elephant, Rani, set off the valve. — AP.

Guardian 17.6.84. [a]

Jakarta, (AFP) – A rogue elephant known as "Broken Tusk" has reappeared in west Sumatra, four years after it killed a woman and rampaged through 74 houses.

The Times 5.7.85. [b]

AMERICA has plenty of regulations for life after world war three — strict banking hours, no extra time to pay the phone bill ... and reserve supplies of nuclear weapons.

The Guardian 5.7.85. [c]

A CATALAN travelling salesman yesterday discovered that he had left the waiters in one of his regular hotels in southern Spain one of the biggest tips of all times — £19,000, *Edward Owen writes from Madrid.*
Mr Jose Ezcurra spent last Wednesday at a hotel in Torredelcampo, and left two state lottery tickets for Saturday's draw. His number came up trumps and now the staff are trying to find out where he is to thank him.

Guardian 9.6.84. [d]

A MAN described by police as a "confused vagabond" used a heavy stone to shatter or damage 86 busts yesterday in the Roman park, Villa Borghese. He was detained while carrying a bag full of noses chipped off the statues. — AP.

Guardian 17.6.84. [e]

Mr John Town and his wife, Shiona, are planning to climb the 14,810-ft Mount Bielukha in the Altai Mountains in western Siberia.

Guardian 25.6.84. [f]

A US team in Boston has devised a method of producing large amounts of human skin in the laboratory which could save the lives of many burns victims.

Guardian 17.8.84. [g]

Rogue's return　　**Couple leave for Russian climb**　　**Life after death**

Sad nose　　**Burns advance**

Tip is just the ticket　　**Hippos die**

110

Unit 21

1 Pairs

Here are three package holidays to St. Lucia in the Caribbean.
Discuss the advantages and disadvantages of each holiday.
Use the first conditional (see page 114):
If we take the Sungate holiday, it'll be cheaper. But if we take the Coots holiday, we'll stay in a luxury hotel.

How many advantages and disadvantages can you think of?
Choose one of the holidays.

FLYAWAY

£900 11 nights

THE COVE HOTEL **

Situated right on the beach, a local centre of night life, with discotheques and beach parties.

Only 2 miles from town.

COOTS

£1,480 14 nights

THE PALACE ****

Superb restaurants with local specialities and international cuisine. Surrounded by beautiful gardens, only 10 minutes walk from town and 2 miles from the beach.

SUNGATE

£835 14 nights

CASTLE TOWER **

In the attractive centre of Castries, with its colourful street markets. Only three miles from the beach.

2 Groups

You live in London.
You are invited to stay in a villa on the Sicilian coast near Palermo. You can stay for any number of days between Saturday 10th July and Sunday 1st August. The accommodation and food are all free. You will only need money for entertainment, eating out, presents, etc. You each have £550 for the holiday. But of that £550, £150 will go on essentials to buy before you go: clothes, holiday insurance, etc.

Decide:

1. How and when you will go.
   How and when you will come back.
2. If you will visit other places on the way, e.g. stay in Rome for two nights on the way home.
3. How much money you will spend. Remember to calculate money for food and hotels on the journey. Cheap hotels in European cities cost a minimum of £20 per person per night.

What are the possible routes?
What are the times of trains/ships/planes?
What are the fares?

Useful Language

If we take a scheduled flight, it'll cost more.
It's cheaper by charter.
But then we'll have to leave on Wednesday 14th.
Why don't we fly to Genoa and then . . . ?
If we do that we'll have . . .
How can we get from . . . to . . . ?
How long will it take by . . . ?
Could we come back a different way?

Use
- the world map
- the timetables (see opposite)
- the advertisements giving prices (see opposite)

Note:
Scheduled airline costs – Alitalia
Milan/Palermo £87.00 o/w £174.00 rtn
Rome/Palermo £56.50 o/w £113.00 rtn

CHARTER TRAVEL

	o/w	rtn
Athens	£71	£135
Alicante	£59	£84
Barcelona	£56	£95
Lisbon	£62	£115
Madrid	£56	£90
Milan	£80	£145
Palermo	£80	£127
Palma	£70	£120
Rome	£90	£160
Salonika	£80	£120

01–437–3236
28 Chapel St., London W2

EXPRESS COACHES

	Singles
Athens	£45
Milan/Venice	£53
Belgrade/Zagreb	£60
Basle	£37

Holiday Bus Co.
36 Green Terrace, SW1
01–629–4364

TRY THE TRAIN

Super discount fares—short period only

Cross Europe	£
London/Genoa	60.50
London/Madrid	49.50
London/Milan	71.00
London/Zagreb	101.70
London/Zurich	71.40

Italy	£
Milan/Palermo	20.34
Rome/Palermo	17.58
Genoa/Milan	3.25
Milan/Rome	13.17

Further information ring 01–436–9247
Or ask your local Travel Agent

Mediterranean Shipping
403 Regent St., London W1
01–420–1349

	CHEAPEST	
	S	R
Majorca/Barcelona	£22	£44
Palermo/Tunis	£17.20	£34.40
Palermo/Genoa	£30	£60
Brindisi/Corfu	£15	£30
Venice/Patras	£95	£190
Naples/Cagliari	£11.20	£22.40
Naples/Palermo	£17.20	£34.40

Holiday Bus Company

		D	A
London/Milan	daily except Sun.	08.00	13.00 (next day)
Milan/London	daily except Tues.	16.30	11.30 (next day)

Med Shipping

		D	A
Palermo/Naples	nightly	20.30	7.30
Naples/Palermo	nightly	20.30	7.30
Genoa/Palermo	nightly	22.30	7.00
Palermo/Genoa	nightly	22.30	7.00

Trains

			D	A
International:	London/Genoa		daily	12.30	10.55 a.m.
	Genoa/London		daily	9.45	8.10 a.m.
Italian:	Milan/Genoa		hourly	6.15	8.15
	Milan/Rome		8.35, 15.45, 19.00	14.35, 21.35, 1.00
	Milan/Palermo		8.35, 15.45, 19.00	8.35, 15.45, 19.00 (next day)
	Genoa/Milan		hourly	06.20	08.20
	Rome/Milan		1.30, 5.45, 11.00	7.30, 11.45, 17.00
	Palermo/Milan		7.30, 11.45, 17.00	7.30, 11.45, 17.00
	Rome/Palermo		14.45, 22.00, 1.30	8.35, 15.45, 19.00
	Palermo/Rome		7.30, 11.45, 17.00	1.45, 5.15, 10.30

European Charters

		D	A
London to Rome	daily	10.30	14.15
London to Palermo	Weds.	23.05	3.05
Rome to London	daily	15.30	17.00
Palermo to London	Thurs.	6.30	8.30

Italian Air

		D	A
Rome to Palermo	daily	20.05	21.05
Milan to Palermo	daily	17.30	19.30
Palermo to Rome	daily	8.00	9.00
Palermo to Milan	daily	13.45	15.45

3 Class

Each group elects a spokesperson. S/he explains how they are going to arrange their holiday.

Language

First conditional

Form

Condition: If + verb in Simple Present *If we fly ...*
Result: will + verb ... *it'll be quicker*

or

Result: *It'll be quicker ...*
Condition: *if we fly ...*

Negative: *If we don't fly, we can go by train and boat.*
If we travel by train, we won't have many days in the villa.

Interrogative: *Will it be cheaper if we fly by charter plane?*

Use

To express 'probable' future events

How questions

We can use *how* to ask questions.
How did you travel? By train.
So *how* asks about 'manner' or the way you do something.

We can use *how* + *many* to ask about 'countable quantities'.
How many people were on the plane? Oh, about 200.

If *how* asks for 'manner' and *how many* asks for 'countable quantities', then match:

1 how much   **a** distance
2 how long   **b** frequency
3 how often   **c** length/duration
4 how far   **d** mass quantities

Write an example for each of the questions.
Give a suitable answer for each.

Simple Present in the future

Use

1 To talk about timetables and to talk about travel in the near future
The Rome train leaves at ...
The train from Genoa gets in at ...

2 With a time adverbial to talk about events in the near future
The bus leaves tomorrow morning at 8.00. It gets into Milan at 13.00 the next day.
Peter gets back tomorrow at 8.00.
I leave on Saturday.

Underline all the time adverbials in the above examples.

Here are some details of a coach/camping holiday from an Australian travel brochure. Use these verbs to complete the text.

to drive, to visit, to travel, to leave, to leave, to explore.

SATURDAY — KINGS CANYON
BLD
Leave Alice Springs and travel to the Henbury Meteorite Craters, then through Wallara Ranch to Reedys Rock Hole and Kings Canyon.

SUNDAY — AYERS ROCK
BLD
Today we ——— through the old Angus Downs Station, pausing at Mt. Connor and Curtain Springs before travelling to 'The Rock'.

MONDAY — AYERS ROCK
BLD
This is another day of adventure as we ——— Ayers Rock and the Olgas.

TUESDAY — ARKARINGA CREEK
BLD
We ——— the Rock and ——— to Curtin Springs cattle station and then on through Mulga Park and Victory Downs Stations to camp.

WEDNESDAY — COOBER PEDY
BLD
Arriving Coober Pedy for lunch, we — the opal caves and underground homes of this fascinating town.

THURSDAY — PORT AUGUSTA
BLD
We ——— Coober Pedy and travel south east past the Salt Pen, Lake Hart and former rocket-launching site of Woomera. Make camp at Port Augusta at the head of the Spencer Gulf.

(Trailfinders, Bill King's Australia (1984))

Vocabulary Look through this unit (page 111 – page 117) and list ten words you want to learn. Choose the words which interest you; the ones which are useful to you. Check the meaning in a dictionary. Write one sentence with each word.

Developments

[A] You are going to visit friends in Australia. You intend to rent a car in Canberra and drive to their home.
This is part of a letter from your friend giving directions. Follow the directions on the map. What is the name of your friend's town?

> You can hire a car quite easily in Canberra, but make sure you get a good one for travelling on bad roads. You'll want to see some scenery so take your time and follow this route. Just outside Canberra to the south take a sharp right turn onto a small back road. It zig-zags up north into the mountains, past a lake and finally takes you to Tumut. From there take route 18 down across the national park to Kiandra in the centre. Turn right there for Cabramurra and follow the signs for Corryong. You could stay the night somewhere around there. Stay on that road - you'll go through Shelley and come to the Murray Valley Highway - route 16. Keep going west: it's quite a long way!
> The turning just before us is to Tongala. Stop at the first telephone you see, give us a ring and I'll direct you to the house.

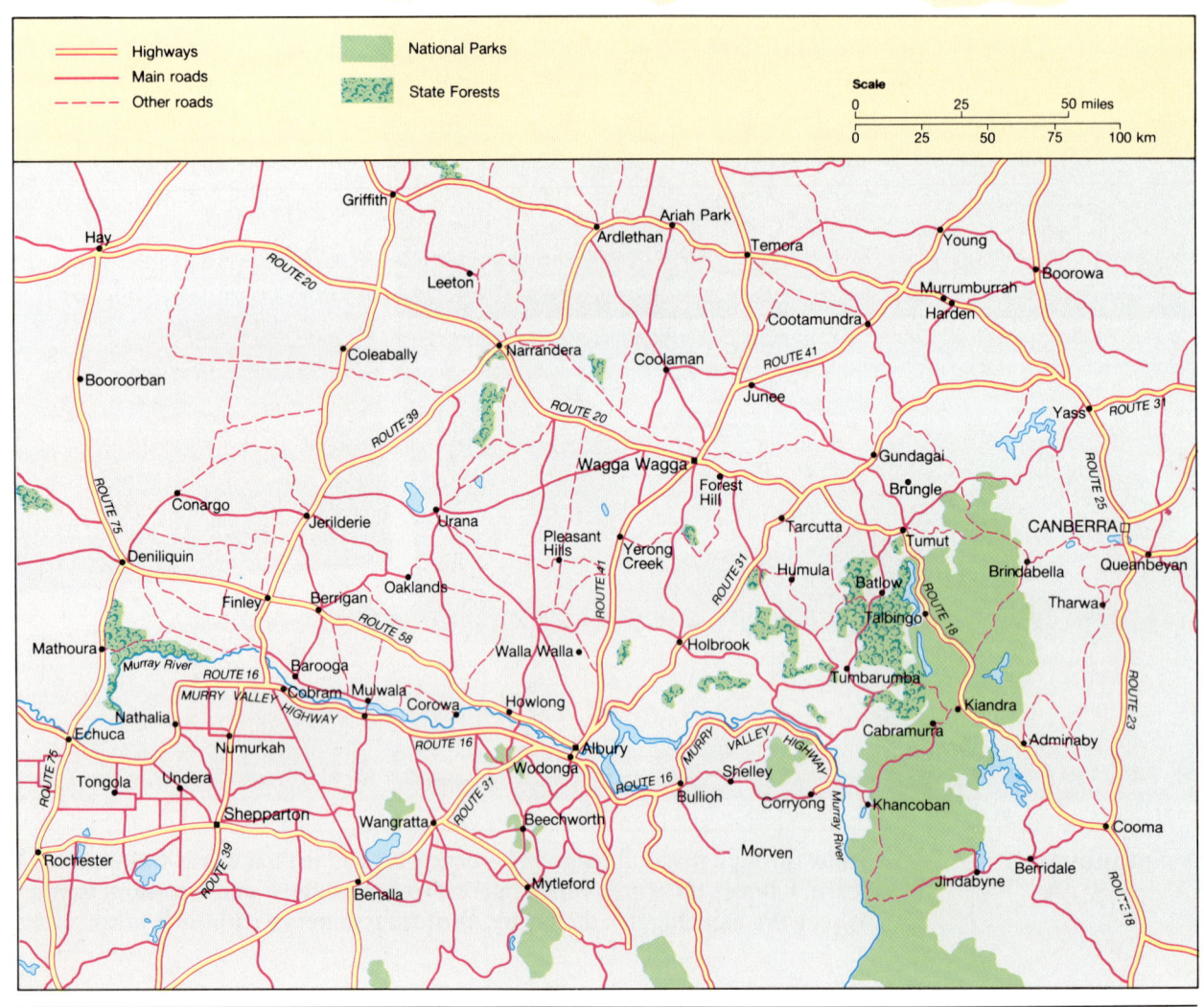

[B] Listen.

Use the pictures and the map and find Vera's house.
Tick ✓ which pictures are correct.
Put a cross X on the map to mark the house.

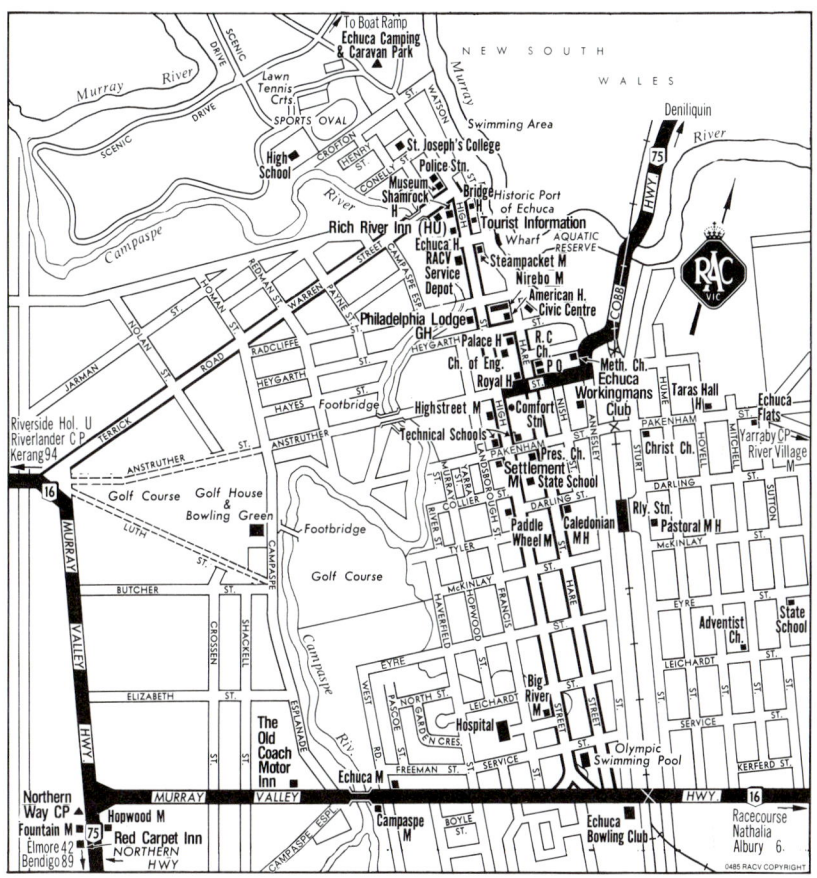

  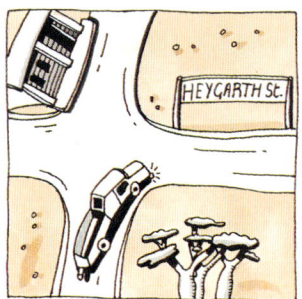 

Unit 22

1 Pairs
List three good things and three bad things about moving house.

2 [A] Read this letter.
What is Elizabeth worried about?
What is her mother worried about?

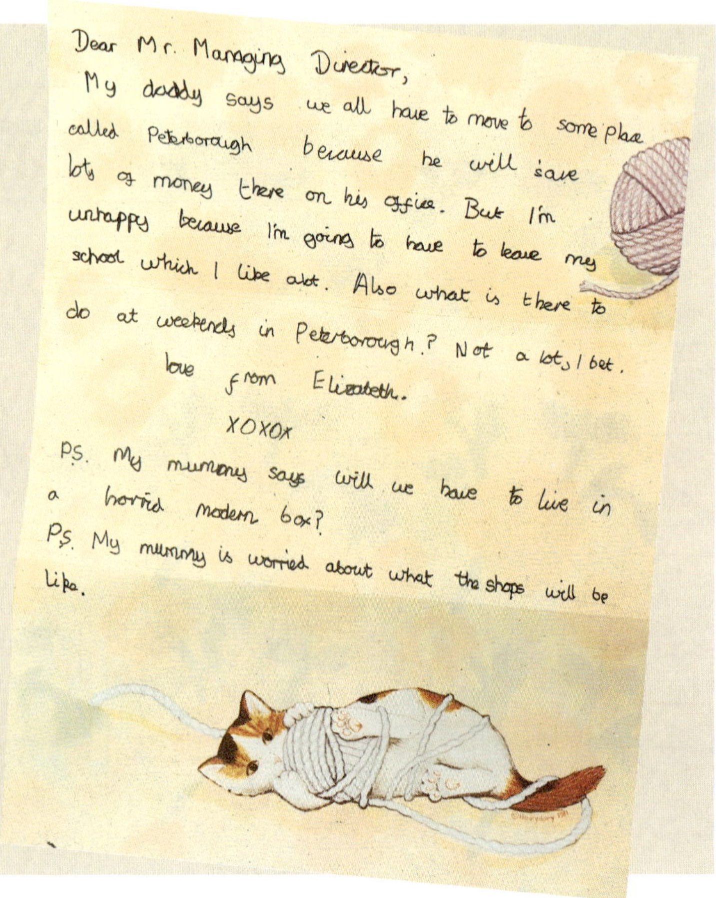

Dear Mr. Managing Director,
My daddy says we all have to move to some place called Peterborough because he will save lots of money there on his office. But I'm unhappy because I'm going to have to leave my school which I like alot. Also what is there to do at weekends in Peterborough? Not a lot, I bet.
     love from Elizabeth.
         xoxox
P.S. My mummy says will we have to live in a horrid modern box?
P.S. My mummy is worried about what the shops will be like.

[B] Pairs

Which of these pictures:
a answer Elizabeth's questions?
b answer her mother's questions?

Write a caption for each picture.

[C] Make notes for a reply to Elizabeth's letter. When you finish, check your notes with the letter on page 120.

3 Listen to this radio advertisement for a town called Milton Keynes. It gives us six points of 'information' about the town. What are they?

Is it a 'good' advert? Will it attract people to the town? Why/Why not?

4 Pairs

Think about your town or the town you are in.
What can the town offer either business people or tourists?
Make a list of business/tourist features.
Make another list of different ways you can tell people about the town.
Write a script for a short radio advertisement, or design a newspaper/magazine advertisement which will tell people about the town.

Useful Language

What has our town got for tourists/business people?
What have we got to offer?
We have to identify the ...
We could stress the ...
We've got to consider transport/hotels/housing ...

5

Don't worry Elizabeth.
Here are some pictures of Peterborough, and there are many more things to do we haven't room to show you. (Bet you didn't know Thomas the Tank Engine lives here.)
And please tell Mummy not to worry about the shops, because our shopping centre is the best in Europe.
Nor about houses, because she'll find lots of lovely old ones as well as new houses here.
And Mummy and Daddy will be able to afford a much nicer one.
Of course you'll have to change your school, and we know that's sad. But children who've moved here love their new schools.
And you won't have to say goodbye to London for ever and ever, because it's only 50 minutes away by train (bet you thought it was miles further).
There's lots to do here all the time.

It even rains less than where you live.
We think you'll like it in Peterborough. After all, your Daddy wouldn't move to a place where you and Mummy would be unhappy, would he?

Please send me your information pack. And show me that Elizabeth's worries are groundless. Telephone John Bouldin on Peterborough (0733) 68931. Or send the coupon to Peterborough Development Corporation, Touthill Close, Peterborough PE1 1UJ. (Telex: 32825).

Name
Company
Position
Address
                                    Tel:

the Peterborough Effect
It works for people. As well as business.

Find another word for 'space'.
Find a verb which means 'have enough money to buy something'.
Find a phrase which means 'for a very long time'.

Language 22

Future obligation

To express future obligation, we use:
will have to – *We will have to advertise on TV.*
going to have to – *He's going to have to answer our questions.*
has/have (got to) – *I have got to see them next week.*

Look again at the letter on page 118. Find an example for each of the three forms in the letter.

Vocabulary

Make a list of all the 'new' verbs you can find in this unit. Check the meanings. Write one sentence for each verb.

Developments

Can you guess what life will be like for you and your children in the next century?

Arthur C. Clarke is a scientist and science fiction writer. He is famous for his accurate predictions. In 1945 he predicted the use of telecommunications satellites. His books include the world-famous '2001 A Space Odyssey'.

This is part of a quiz from the American science magazine 'Omni'—July 1985. Omni asked Arthur C. Clarke for his answers to some questions about our future world. His answers are on page 141. How do you see the future? Answer the questions. Compare your answers with Arthur C. Clarke's.

1 When will an ordinary person be able to buy a ride on a space flight?

   a by 1995
   b by 2000
   c by 2010
   d by 2020
   e after 2020

2 Will we make contact with extraterrestials (living creatures from other worlds) in the 21st century?

   a Yes
   b No

3 Which of these events will occur first in space?

   a a birth
   b a marriage
   c a murder
   d a suicide

4 In 2010 how many years will you add to your life with life-extension drugs (drugs to make you live longer)?

a none
b 1–3
c 5
d 10
e 20
f over 25

5 Name the most common energy source in the next century.

a oil
b coal
c fusion
d fission
e solar power
f geothermal power

6 Which will be the most polluted city on earth in the year 2000?

a Tokyo
b Los Angeles
c Rio
d New York
e Mexico City
f Shanghai
g São Paolo
h Calcutta

7 Which city will have the biggest population in the year 2000?

a Shanghai
b Los Angeles
c Tokyo
d Rio de Janeiro
e Mexico City
f New York
g São Paolo
h Calcutta

8 Which nation will first set up a permanent space colony?

a USA
b China
c A European group of nations
d USSR
e There will never be a permanent space colony.

9 On New Years Eve (December 31) 1999 how many people will drink champagne in space?

a none
b 1–9
c 10–20
d 21–50
e 51–100
f 101–1000
g more than 1000

10 By the year 2000 how many nations will have workable nuclear weapons?

a 8–10
b 11–13
c 14–18
d 19–24
e more than 25

11 What fuel will cars run on in 2010?

a petrol
b gassohol (a type of alcohol)
c electricity
d steam

12 Today there are approximately 4.5 billion people in the world. How many will there be in the year 2000?

a 5–6 (×billion)
b 6–7
c 7–8
d 8–9
e 9–10
f over 10

13 What will a classroom of the 21st century be like?

a A group of students in school listening to a human teacher.
b A group of students in school listening to a robot or computer teacher.
c Each student at home with a computer terminal.

14 What will 21st century people say was the greatest invention or discovery of the 20th century?

a The computer
b The theory of relativity
c Polio vaccine
d Splitting the atom
e Television
f The satellite

15 What will be the most difficult, perhaps impossible, challenge in the 21st century?

a Stopping 'hunger' in the world.
b Reducing and eliminating nuclear weapons.
c Finding different energy sources.
d Stabilizing the world population.
e Colonizing outer space.

Unit 23

1

Diary entries (February 1988):
- Mon 1 — Interviews for area sales manager
- Tue 2 — Interviews
- Wed 3 — Interviews
- Mon 8 — Glasgow – see new factory
- Tue 9 — Glasgow
- Wed 10 — Glasgow
- Wed 17 — Rio Conference starts
- Thu 18 — Rio
- Fri 19 — Rio
- Sat 20 — Rio
- Sun 21 — Rio
- Mon 22 — Rio
- Tue 23 — Last day of conference

Note: We need a ½ day meeting to select applicant – following the interviews? To: S.D. + P.M.

File stamps: CONFIDENTIAL / PERSONNEL / Job Application

S. Freeman is the managing director (MD) of a large company with central offices in London. The company has a factory in Oxford and they are opening a new one in Glasgow. S. Freeman often works with D. Wilkins, the sales director (SD), and J. Lyons, the personnel manager (PM).

Look at the picture of S. Freeman's desk top.

a He has to go on three trips.
Where to?   1 _Rio_   Why?   1 _Conference_
            2 _____   2 _____
            3 _____   3 _____

b He has to interview people. Who with? _____ What for? _____

c He has to give a report. Who to? _____ What about? _____

d He has to attend four meetings.
What are they? _____   Who are they with? _____

23

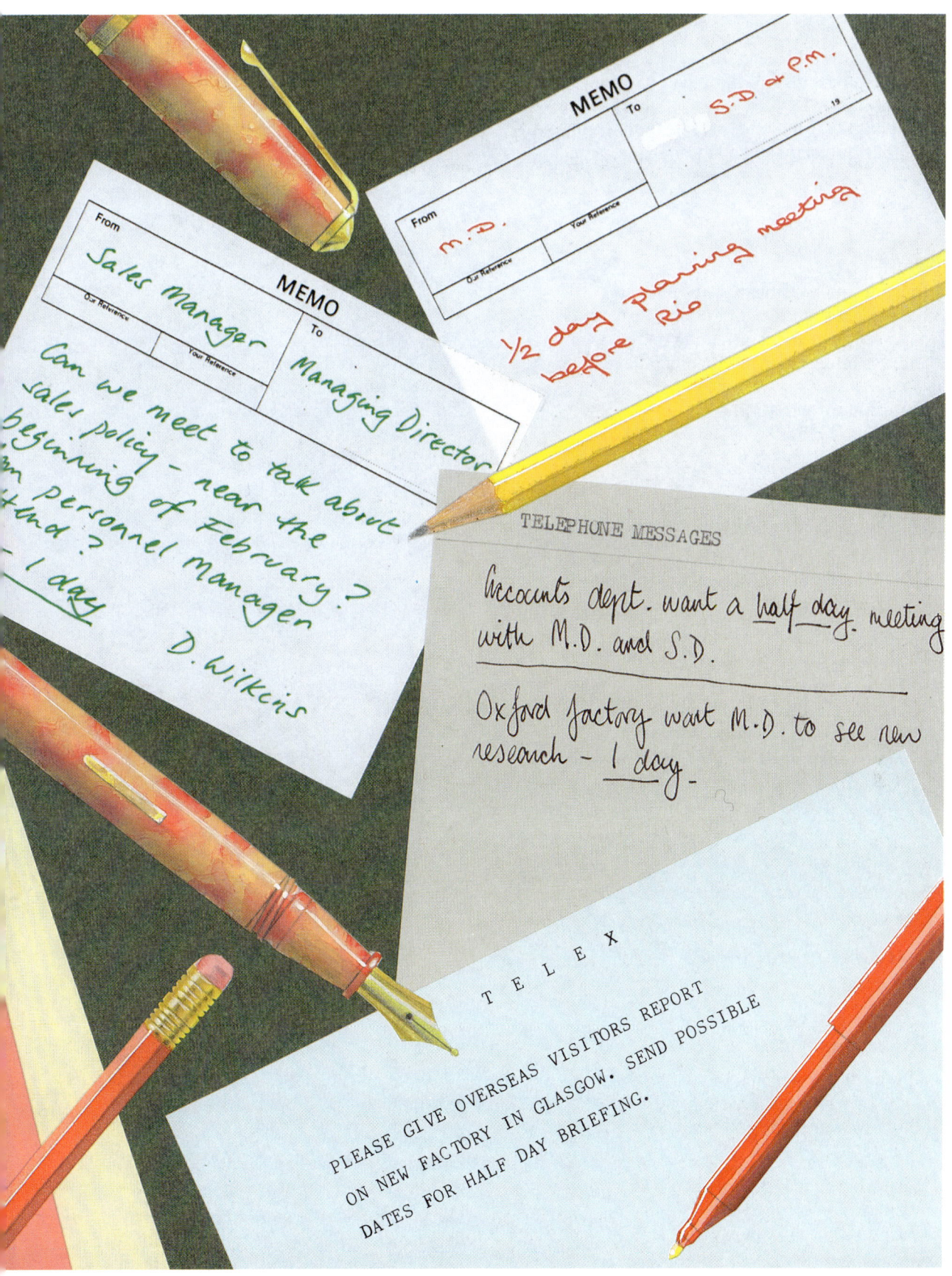

23

2 Listen.

What are Freeman, Wilkins and Lyons discussing?
Listen again. Find one example for each of the four 'futures' shown in Language, page 127.

3 Groups

Imagine you are Freeman, Wilkins and Lyons. Look at the planner for February on page 124. Use the information on the desk and this information to complete the planner.

Personal information

Managing Director:
You want at least five free days and you want to spend three or more of them with your family.

Sales Director:
You will be away from the office on business from Monday 8th to Thursday 11th inclusive.

Personnel Manager:
You will be away from the office on Wednesday 3rd, Thursday 11th, and Friday 26th.

```
Oxford   - hourly trains to and from London.
Glasgow  - daily flights to and from London. Allow half a day.
           daily/nightly trains to and from London. Allow half a
           day or a night.
Rio      - daily flights to and from London. Allow 24 hours for
           travel.
```

Did you know it's Carnival in Rio from Monday 22rd to Friday 26th?

Useful Language

Why don't you go to ... on the ...?
Then you can do ...
You could travel overnight/by plane/by train.
How about meeting on the ...?
No, that won't work because ...
When are you ...?
Will we all have to be there?
What are you going to ...?

Week	One	Two	Three	Four
Mon	1	8	15	22 Rio
Tues	2 Job interviews (PM & SI)	9 Glasgow	16	23 Rio
Wed	3	10 Glasgow	17	24 Rio end of conference
Thurs	4 Job interviews (PM & SI)	11	18 Rio Conference	25
Fri	5	12	19 Rio	26
Sat	6	13	20 Rio	27
Sun	7	14	21 Rio	28

4 Plan your next year.

Think of your personal life
    your work/study
    your home and family

In the next year:
What will you have to do?
What are you going to do?
What do you think you will do?
Makes notes for each of the above.

Groups
Compare your plans.
Do any of you have similar plans/intentions?
Or are they very different?
Decide who has the most ambitious plan.
Decide who will have the most difficult year.
Decide who has the most optimistic plan.

Language

The future

There is no future tense form in English.
There are several ways of expressing future time.

Form

1 *will* + verb
One day we'll go there.
I'm certain she'll be the next president.
So, we'll meet on Tuesday at 10 a.m.
I promise I'll do it.

2 *going to* + verb
I'm going to leave my family.
It's going to rain.

3 Present Continuous in the future
We're visiting friends this weekend.

4 Simple Present in the future
The plane leaves at 6.00 on Friday.

Use

1 Prediction; general indefinite future; instant decisions; promises
2 Intentions already decided; prediction of near future
3 Events definitely arranged, usually with time adverbial
4 Travel and timetables, usually with time adverbial

Preposition + *-ing*

When a verb follows a preposition it takes the *ing* form: verb + *ing*.
(For spelling, see present participle spelling on page 61.)

Prepositions: after, before, to, on, etc.
We look forward to seeing you soon.
Before leaving he inspected the new laboratory.
After visiting the factory he'll have to write a report.

Vocabulary

Look through this unit and make a list of all the words which look similar to a word in your language. Check the meaning carefully. Write sentences for the English words.

Developments

When you write a letter to a friend or relative you can write it any way you like. Here is an exercise to help you write more formal letters.

Layout

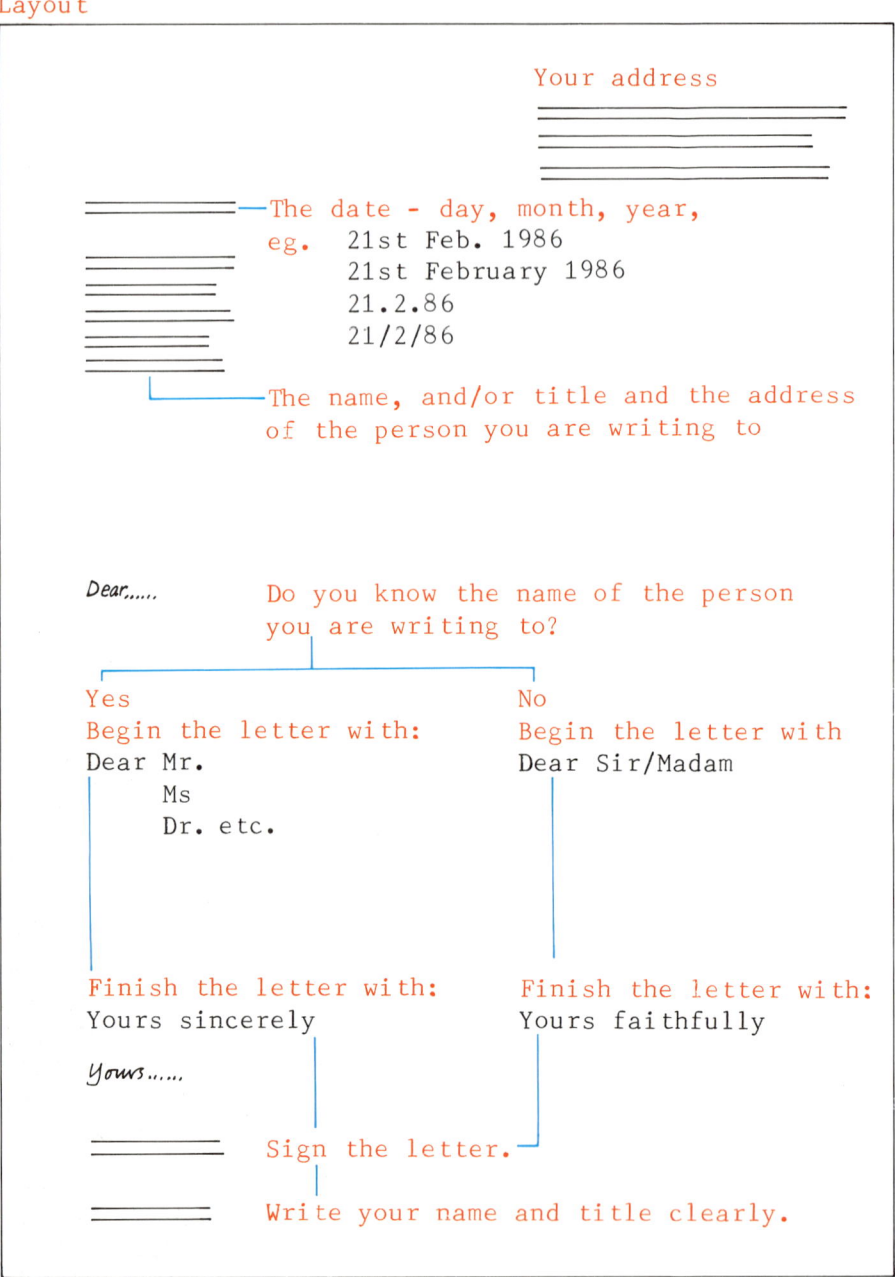

Listen.

You will hear two business letters dictated.
1 Listen to the first one.
   Who is it to?
   What is it about?

Now write it down: play, stop, and play the tape as much as you like. Use the above layout but first write *your* address at the top of the letter.

2 Do the same with the second one.

Unit 24

1 Pairs

How do these five components make a story? Invent one. Make notes about it – do *not* write the story.

Try telling the story to each other. Try to make it interesting/dramatic.

Tell your story to the rest of the class. Listen to their stories.

- a Jumbo jet
- a 2 month old baby girl
- a young 20 year old woman
- a search
- a polecat

2 Listen.

This is the 'real' story. It happened in 1984. How many points are the same in your story? Who has the closest version to the one on the tape?

24

3 Pairs

Choose two characters, one place, one object and one action.
Invent a story using all five components.
Write only notes. Practise telling your story to each other.
Tell the class your story.
Listen to theirs.

Actions:

a laugh
a scream
a fight
a decision

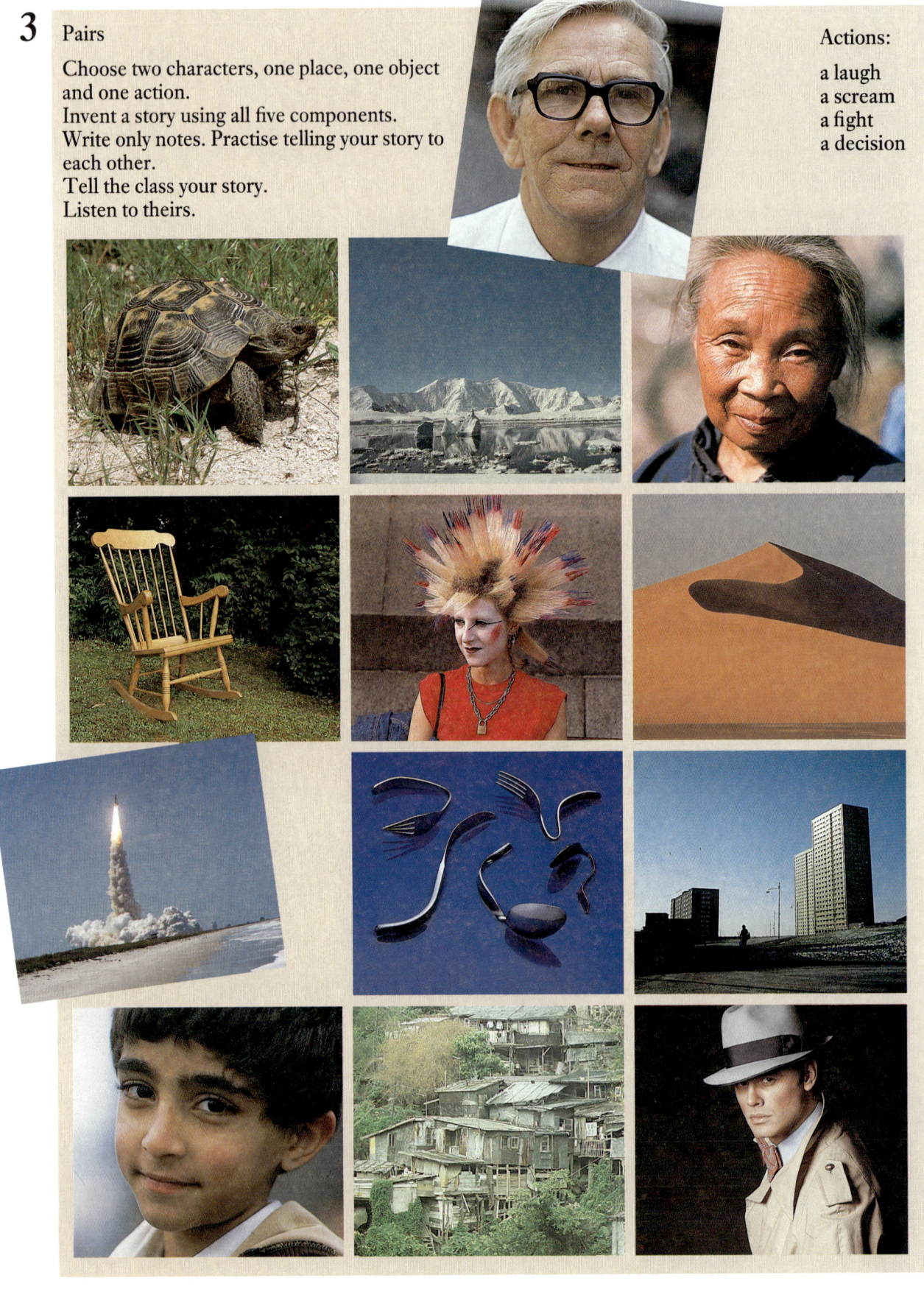

Language

24

The past:

In Book 1 we have looked at the past of *to be*, and at two tenses which we use to talk about the past: the Simple Past and the Past Continuous. A summary is below.

Form

a *to be*
   is/are = was/were | *She was in Geneva last week.*
   He was very hungry.

b The Simple Past
   Regular: verb + *ed*   *lived, worked, happened.*
   Irregular: go — *went*   see — *saw*   leave — *left*
   come — *came*   do — *did*   give — *gave.*

c The Past Continuous | *She was speaking at a conference.*
   was/were + verb *ing* | *They were working all night.*

Use

The Simple Past

1 For things/events that happened at a time that is now finished
   We saw them last week.
2 For events that are clearly finished, but time is not stated
   The American Civil War divided the country.
3 To tell stories
   Inspector Trouvé got on the first train. He had to hurry . . .

The Past Continuous

1 To talk about things that were happening at a time in the past
   At that moment he was sleeping.   At 5.00 pm they were working.
2 To describe a scene (often continuing with the Simple Past to say what happened next)
   It was a very cold night. People were hurrying home; some were trying to get on buses, some were doing some late shopping. Nobody really noticed the plane. But they all stopped when they . . .
3 To describe a long action that was taking place when a quick event happened/occurred
   They were watching TV when the police rang the door bell.

There are other ways to talk about the past in English. They are looked at later in the course.

Vocabulary

Choose one picture of a person and one of a place. Name the items.
Put a suitable adjective before each one.

Developments

[A] Look at these headlines.

Polecat in jumbo jet rumpus

Is 'a rumpus'
– an animal?
– a disturbance?
– a kind of aeroplane?

SORRY MUM!

I knew I wasn't on the Isle of Man when I saw the dolphins

By ALISTER MARTIN

TEENAGE stowaway Andrew Bolton talked yesterday about his "day trip" to the Isle of Man that ended in Egypt.

Safe home after his flight from Cairo, Andrew hugged his parents and said: "I knew something was wrong when I saw dolphins and blue sky."

Do you think 'I' is
– Andrew?
– his father?
– his mother?

Find the Isle of Man on a map.

Do you think this article will be about
– someone who bought a dolphin?
– someone who went away on a boat?
– someone who likes dolphins?

Glossary

to doze – to sleep lightly
rabies – a 'killer' disease spread by animals
freighter – a ship which carries 'things' not passengers
to plead guilty – to say 'I did it' in a court
stowaway – someone who hides on a ship or plane without paying
bound for – on the way to 'somewhere'
gaol – prison
the crew – the people who work on a ship or plane
docks – harbour; place where ships arrive, etc.
to make a bid for independence – to try to get free
Manx (adj.) from the Isle of Man
to admit responsibility – to say you did something
alert – a warning or alarm

[B] The two stories are mixed up.
Find the story to go with each headline.
Put the stories in the correct order.

[7] A POLECAT running loose among more than 400 passengers aboard a jumbo jet flying to Gatwick airport in London caused confusion yesterday, and last night landed Sharon Roper, aged 20, in gaol for a month.

[6] In fact he was on board Greek freighter the Eliot, bound for Australia and not making a stop until Port Said, 3000 miles away.

[5] Andrew, who brought his mother a toy camel, added: "I wasn't trying to run away. I just wanted a day out."

[10] Andrew, 16, disappeared two weeks ago. He went to the docks near his home in Heysham, Lancs, and stowed away on what he thought was the Manx ferry.

[3] The polecat was hidden in her hand luggage when she boarded a People Express jet bound for England from Newark, New Jersey, and it made its own bid for independence when the aircraft was 30,000 feet above Scotland.

[4] Later she appeared before a special magistrates court at Crawley, Sussex, where she pleaded guilty to contravening the rabies laws.

[13] All the passengers were ordered to stay aboard the aircraft until the hunt for the animal ended, and then each of them was searched before Ms Roper admitted responsibility for taking the polecat on board.

[11] Ms Roper, an unmarried mother, from Upper Marlboro, Maryland, US, was sentenced to a month's imprisonment or a £700 fine with £50 costs. She elected to go to gaol.

[1] The crew radioed the alert, and police and animal experts were standing by when the aircraft landed.

[14] Ms Roper nursing her two-month-old baby daughter, Samia, was dozing when the polecat escaped, and passengers were terrified when the animal, with its needle-sharp teeth run among them.

[2] Andrew was put on the first flight home from Port Said—and his parents, Elizabeth and John, had to pay his £170 fare.

Luck

[9] The crew found the boy hiding in a lifeboat on the second day out. They notified the police who told his parents.

[12] Mrs Bolton said "We're just relieved he's home—and pleased he's not in any trouble."

[8] "The crew told me a stowaway brought good luck," he said.

[C] Look at the stowaway article on page 135. Look at the verbs. Find the verbs for communication. Write one in each bubble.

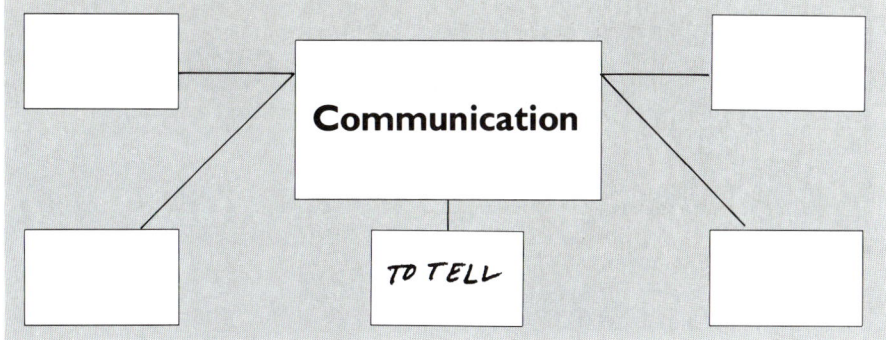

[D] Look at the polecat article on page 135.
Find an expression meaning 'to be very frightened'.
Find the verb which means to go from 'in the air' to 'on the ground'.
Find a synonym for 'aeroplane'.
Find a word meaning 'the rules of a country'.
There is a printing error in this article. Can you find it?

We refer to this world map in a number of activities.

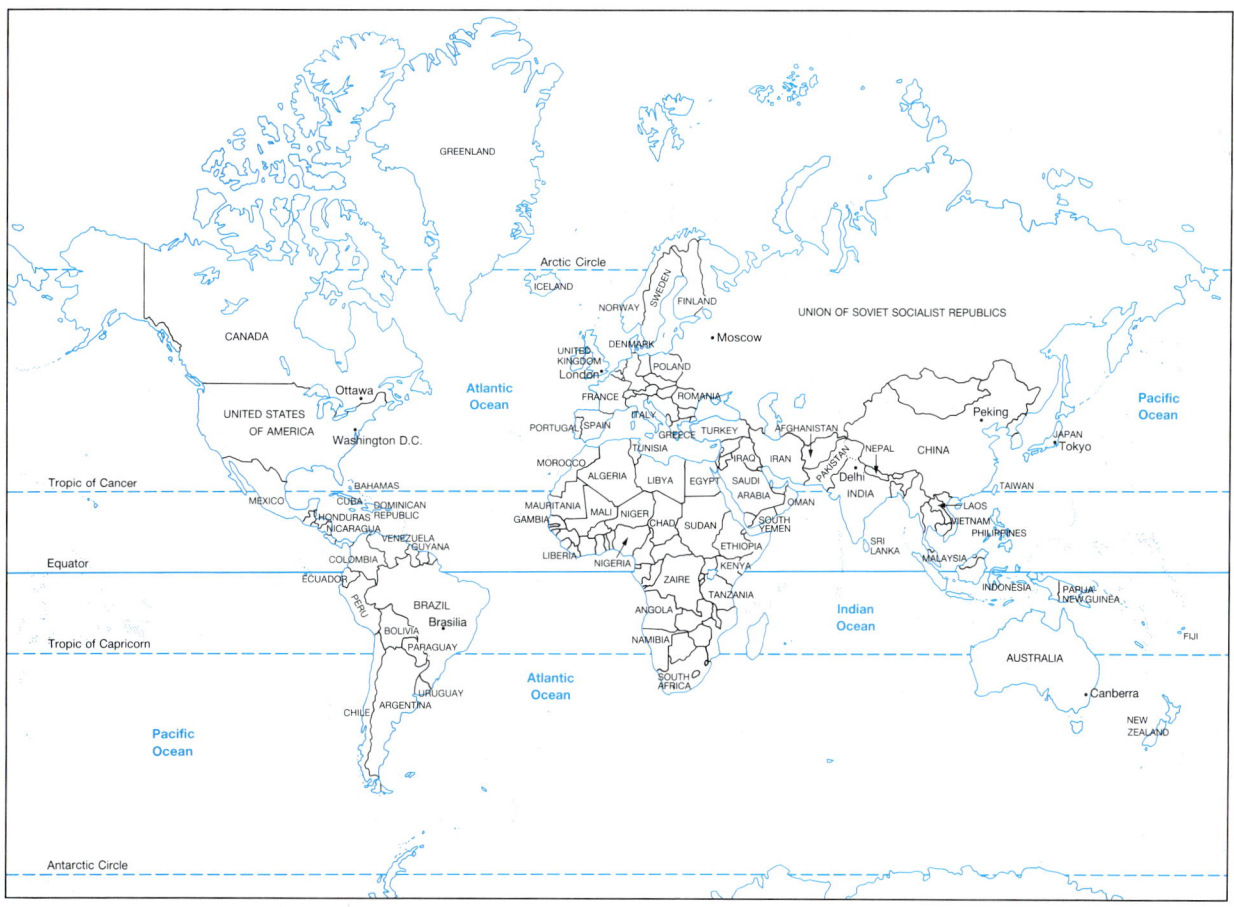

TEENAGE stowaway Andrew Bolton talked yesterday about his "day trip" to the Isle of Man that ended in Egypt.

Safe home after his flight from Cairo, Andrew hugged his parents and said: "I knew something was wrong when I saw dolphins and blue sky."

Andrew, who brought his mother a toy camel, added: "I wasn't trying to run away. I just wanted a day out."

Andrew, 16, disappeared two weeks ago. He went to the docks near his home in Heysham, Lancs, and stowed away on what he thought was the Manx ferry.

In fact he was on board a Greek freighter the Eliot, bound for Australia and not making a stop until Port Said, 3000 miles away.

Luck

The crew found the boy hiding in a lifeboat on the second day out. They notified the police who told his parents.

"The crew told me a stowaway brought good luck," he said.

Andrew was put on the first flight home from Port Said—and his parents, Elizabeth and John, had to pay his £170 fare.

Mrs Bolton said "We're just relieved he's home—and pleased he's not in any trouble."

Polecat in jumbo jet rumpus

A POLECAT running loose among more than 400 passengers aboard a jumbo jet flying to Gatwick airport in London caused confusion yesterday, and last night landed Sharon Roper, aged 20, in gaol for a month.

The polecat was hidden in her hand luggage when she boarded a People Express jet bound for England from Newark, New Jersey, and it made its own bid for independence when the aircraft was 30,000 feet above Scotland.

Ms Roper nursing her two-month-old baby daughter, Samia, was dozing when the polecat escaped, and passengers were terrified when the animal, with its needle-sharp teeth run among them.

The crew radioed the alert, and police and animal experts were standing by when the aircraft landed.

All the passengers were ordered to stay aboard the aircraft until the hunt for the animal ended, and then each of them was searched before Ms Roper admitted responsibility for taking the polecat on board.

Later she appeared before a special magistrates court at Crawley, Sussex, where she pleaded guilty to contravening the rabies laws.

Ms Roper, an unmarried mother, from Upper Marlboro, Maryland, US, was sentenced to a month's imprisonment or a £700 fine with £50 costs. She elected to go to gaol.

135

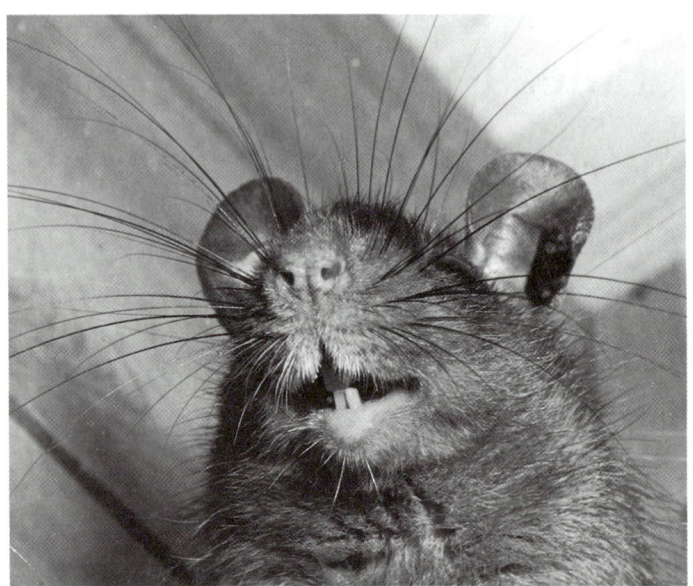

Key

Unit 1

Language

Contractions:
a is **b** has **c** has **d** is

What:
1 c **2** a **3** e **4** b **5** d

We think the colours are:
bright red   – d
red   – b
sort of red – a and e
dark blue   – b or e
light blue   – a

Possessive Adjectives:
1 d **2** a **3** c **4** b **5** e **6** g **7** f

Word Order:
We can say *a cheap watch*
Rule: article + adjective + noun

Unit 2

Language

Plural nouns:
children, women, teeth

Articles B   a, a, a, the, a, the, a, the, a

C **1 an** apple, elephant, hour, orange, ice-cream, uncle, island

2 a bed, sofa, university, door, unit, horse, union, kitchen

Unit 3

Language

Possession:
2 *Rule:* Noun + s + apostrophe (')
3 *Rule:* Noun + apostrophe + s

Developments

[A] **2** Drive **3** Turn **4** Press/Push **5** Close the windows

[B] **a** 1 or 2; **b** 3; **c** 1 or 2; **d** 5; **e** 4

[C] **1** picture, television, record player, doors, plant, books, bookcase, chair, desk, computer, telephone, window, armchair, carpet, settee, cushions, flowers, vase, ashtray, glasses, table

2 Bathroom: nailbrush, toothbrush, towel, razor
Kitchen: saucepan, cup, knife, spoon
Bedroom: bed, alarm clock, pyjamas, pillow
s<u>au</u>cepan, al<u>ar</u>m, p<u>i</u>llow, r<u>a</u>zor, <u>bath</u>room, <u>bed</u>room

Unit 4

Language

Question words:
what – things; *where* – place; *when* – time; *why* – reason; *who* – person; *how* – way/manner; *which* – choice

Who:
a Maggie
b Ronnie
c Who drives Charles to work?
d Who does Diana drive to work?

How:
1 c **2** a **3** d **4** b
Rule: How + adjective + verb phrase.

How often:
once or twice a week; never; every week; just sometimes

Developments

[A] opens, falls, puts, lights, heats, drives, takes, tells, eats

Unit 5

Language

Word Order:
1 a object subject verb
   b verb subject object
   c subject verb object
   d verb object
   Correct – **c**
   Rule: subject verb object

2 a subject auxiliary object verb
   b auxiliary subject verb object
   c verb subject object
   d object verb subject
   Correct – **b**
   Rule: auxiliary subject verb object?

3 a subject auxiliary *not* verb object
   b subject auxiliary object *not* verb
   c object verb auxiliary *not* subject
   Correct – **a**
   Rule: subject auxiliary *not* verb object

Developments

[B] September, April, June, November, February
Every four years. Example: 1984

Unit 6

Language

Adverbs:
Rule: adjective + *ly* = adverb

Word Order:
Rule: verb + *really/very/awfully* + adverb

Possessive pronouns:
1 c **2** a **3** f **4** d **5** g **6** b **7** e

Vocabulary:
a, the, can, picture, have, help, tell, how, ask for, talk about, express, take, I/you/she, etc., my/your, etc.

Developments

[A] **a** 6 **b** 5 **c** 2 **d** 1 **e** 3 **f** 4
[B] **i** c **ii** c **iii** c
[C] circus, Friday, café, 6 o'clock

137

Unit 7

Activity 1: tapescript

1st woman	My ... Look!
1st man	Good heavens, there's a car in the water!
2nd woman	I don't believe it!
2nd man	Oh, no. What can we do?
1st woman	Get, get some ropes.
2nd woman	Ropes, yes.
1st woman	And then we can throw them out.
1st man	Well, hang on. Why don't we, um, um ... Look, I can swim.
2nd woman	No, don't be stupid. The water's too strong.
1st woman	No, that wouldn't work at all. Come on.
2nd woman	Look, we must do something. Let's, let's phone the rescue service.
2nd man	Yeh, yeh.
1st man	We could, we could try ... You see that tree.
1st woman	Yes.
1st man	Well, we can cut it down.
2nd man	Right. I've got an axe.
2nd woman	Oh.
1st man	And then the tree will hit the roof.
1st woman	So then they could climb out on the tree. Right, I get you.
1st man	Yeh, well that's the idea anyway.
2nd woman	Yes, it might work.
2nd man	Look, hang on, why not tie that rope around my waist. Look, look, like this.
1st woman	And you swim out.
1st man	No, no.
2nd woman	You're crazy.
2nd man	Why not?
2nd woman	You can't do that.
1st man	You can't do it. You can't.
2nd man	Then what do we do?
1st woman	Think of something. I know ... telephone. Like I said, we could phone the rescue services ...
2nd man	Yeh, let's do that.
1st woman	... and they could get a helicopter.
1st man	She's right, you know.
2nd man	Yeh, yeh. Go on.
1st man	She's right. Go on.
1st woman	Go on, quick, or they'll drown.
2nd woman	Quick!
2nd man	And run!

Language

Prepositions:
at 2 o'clock   on Wednesday
at the weekend   in the evening
on January 21st   in April 1926
in 1976   on May Day
at night   on his/her birthday

Developments

a Arrivals:
  British Airways   flight BA 215 Tokyo
  Qantas   flight QA 319 Sydney

b Mr Brown to Information Desk.
  Mr & Mrs Smith to Duty Free Shop.
  Sen. Diaz to Information Desk.
  M. Dubois to Hertz Car Hire.

c Gate   Destination   Flight No.
   1   New York   VA 325
   2   Athens   OA 139
   3   Palma   DA 3018
   5   Barcelona   BY 2019

Unit 8

Language

Vocabulary:
economical, big, high, small, fast, cheap, easy, expensive, attractive, comfortable, practical, local, luxury, old, white, quick, good, bad, new, long distance, sports, family, slow, simple, shocking pink, mobile, red, blue, friendly, polite, rude

Developments

[A] Firsts:
The world's first plane
The first manned rocket to the moon
One of the first steam trains

Superlatives:
The world's largest airship
The largest telecommunications satellite
The tallest cactus
One of the world's heaviest men
The singer with the most recording awards
The world's highest mountain
The world's fastest airliner
The world's fastest car
The largest marrow
The highest pole vault
The world's tallest man
The world's smallest woman
The largest and heaviest animal (blue whale)
The largest flying creature (pterosaur)
The longest cable suspension bridge (Humber bridge, UK)
The deepest canyon (Grand Canyon, USA)

[B] o/w = one way or single
rtn = return
Venice: Europ-bus £53.00
Canada: 4 agencies
Morocco: Long Expeditions

Unit 9

Language

Too/enough:
[A] 1 c   2 b   3 a
[B] 1 Because she's too young/she's not old enough.
    2 Because it's too big/it's not small enough.
    3 Because he isn't strong enough/he's too weak/small.

Developments

[A] Shopping list:
half a dozen eggs, a large carton of cream, lettuce, olives, ham, half a dozen oranges

[B] Containers:
box, bottle, jar, plate, bowl, (salt) pot

[C] Expressions of quantity:
some olives, a few mushrooms, How many tomatoes?, half a pound, a couple, three or four, lots (of it), any lettuce, How much, three to four slices, There's enough spaghetti, a bit of butter, some fresh oranges, Is that enough?

Unit 10

Language

Contractions:
1 can't, won't, isn't, doesn't, aren't, hasn't
2 She's, They're, I've, We've, You're
   Do you watch T.V.? a, b, d are possible answers
   Have you got a video? a, c, d are possible answers

Vocabulary:
when, what, time, if, become, superstition, believe, way, think, speak, listen, understand, learn, must, find, word

Developments

[A] The middle picture is correct.

[B] a 4: married, marvellous, masculine, massive
   b 5
   c masculine
   d married
   e marsh, mass, match
   f mat
   g marmalade
   h on a boat; in a radio station
   i massive
   j mask

Unit 11

Language

Simple Present/Present Continuous:
2 and 3 are correct
1 The sun rises every day.
4 Water usually condenses in cold air.
5 The standard of living is rising at the moment.

Spelling:
1 *Rule:* Take the base verb and add *-ing.*
2 *Rule:* ... double the last consonant and add *-ing.*
3 *Rule:* ... drop the *-e* and add *-ing.*

Developments

Stations:
Platform 1
Time: 14.12
Destination: Oxford
No. of stops: 2 (Reading, Oxford)

Platform 2
Time: 15.04
Destination: Reading
No. of stops: 7 (Ealing Broadway, Slough, Burnham, Taplow, Maidenhead, Twyford, Reading)
Notes: Marlow passengers change at Maidenhead

Platform 3
Time: 14.50
Destination: Cheltenham
No. of stops: —
Notes: Platform alteration

Platform 4
Time: 14.00
Destination: Cardiff
No. of stops: 7 (Slough, Reading, Didcot, Swindon, Bristol Parkway, Newport, Cardiff Central)
Notes: 17 minutes late (signal failure at Swindon)

Platform 5
Time: 14.45
Destination: Plymouth
No. of stops: 10 (Reading, Newbury, Westbury, Taunton, Exeter, Dawlish, Teignmouth, Newton Abbot, Totnes, Plymouth)

Unit 12

Language

What was it like?
Barcelona: It's a great city. *or*
Hundreds of tourists and lots to see.
The film: It was very funny. *or*
The acting was terrific.

Developments

[A] 1 e 2 b 3 c 4 g 5 h 6 a 7 d 8 f

[B] hotel – 5; station – 4; airport – 3; car – 6; home – 1; work – 2

[C] 1 Transport: car, bus, bicycle, train, shuttle, plane
   Jobs: computer programmer, cashier, writer, astronaut, mechanic, porter
   Buildings: house, cinema, office block, garage, bank, station
   2 a to think
     b quickly
     c to eat
     d cup
     wet/dry, anxious/relaxed, quickly/slowly, expensive/cheap, cool/warm, large/small

[D] a the people who speak English
   b all the countries which use English as a second language
   c *it* line 1 = *English* line 1
     it line 6 = *English* line 5
   d the majority of the inhabitants of English-speaking countries

Unit 13

Language

Some/any/every compounds:
nobody   nothing   nowhere
anybody   anything   anywhere
somebody   something   somewhere
everybody   everything   everywhere

Developments

1 disappearance
2 somebody who lives after a difficult time
3 bits and pieces from a boat or plane
4 overboard
5 rescued, destroyed, found
6 Spacenapping (normally kidnapping). It means taking somebody into space, when they do not want to go, as a prisoner.
7 extraterrestrials
8 to occur

Unit 14

Activity 1: tapescript
Remember 'em. Why yes, siree, I sure do. They were the two most notorious outlaws we had in them days. Those were the days of the great depression: the 1930s. Bonnie and Clyde travelled all around these southern states. They robbed a lot of shops and banks. They weren't much good though: their robberies often failed, and they murdered anyone that got in their way.

On 11 October 1932, Bonnie and Clyde arrived in the town of Sherman, Texas. It was early afternoon and the streets were empty. Slowly they parked their Ford V8 outside the general store. Bonnie stayed in the car with a shotgun and watched the street. Clyde walked into the store. He ordered some Bologne sausage and some cheese, and waited while the storekeeper cut them. When the storekeeper handed him the sausage and cheese, Clyde pulled out a pistol and demanded money. The storekeeper picked up a meat knife. Clyde shot him and took 28 dollars. Clyde dashed out of the shop and Bonnie started the car. Bonnie and Clyde roared off in a cloud of dust.

Finally, after twelve murders and two years on the run, the police ambushed Bonnie and Clyde. A group of policemen waited by the highway for two days. When Bonnie and Clyde drove past, the police filled them full of bullets.

Language

Spelling:
[A] *Rule:* Take the base of the verb and add *ed*.
[B] *Rule:* For verbs which end in *e* add *d*.
[C] *Rule:* ... change the *y* into *i* and add *ed*.
[D] *Rule:* ... double the last consonant and add *ed*.

Irregulars: go/went, buy/bought, see/saw, come/came
got, had, left, made, put, ran, chose

Developments

[A]
Bubbly Britain   – c
Air deal   – b
Unfortunate   – d
Fatal choice   – i
Twins again   – f
Hairy record   – a
Square one   – h
Rung off   – e
War on pigeons   – g

Unit 15

Language

Verb + *like*:
2 It smells like a flower/perfume.
3 It sounds like an argument/someone.
4 It looks like a UFO/rain.
5 It tastes like a 1932/Bulgarian wine.
6 It feels like a glass/glass.

Vocabulary:
good, thick, fantastic, different, many, old (age), fascinating, quite enormous, very beautiful, hot, ugly, unpleasant, long, tiring, very big, ultra-modern, old (long time), true, lovely, cool, amazing

Developments

[A] 17.7.84   2 4.7.84   3 20.6.84
    4 30.6.84

[B] Dallas → Denver (air) → Boulder (car) → Ouray (car) → Durango (car) → Mesa Verde (car) → Grand Canyon → Las Vegas (car) → San Francisco (car)

[C] 1 Dallas   2 Boulder   3 Ouray
    4 Mesa Verde   5 Grand Canyon
    6 San Francisco

  1 worked at a conference
  2 stayed with friends/walked in the mountains
  3 visited goldmine
  4 visited caves and an Indian reservation
  5 watched a thunder storm
  6 visited Chinatown/rode cable cars/crossed the Golden Gate Bridge

Unit 16

Developments

[A] escaped, crashed, fell, happened, saved, thought, looked, had
  a *I couldn't believe my ears.* meaning 'I didn't believe what I heard'.
  b (i) no (ii) yes (iii) even
  c checkupp (should be *check-up*)

[B] I was getting into my car when I saw the Escort career forward. It seemed to be out of control and crashed straight through the safety barrier. I ran to the edge and looked down. The car was about twenty feet below on a roof and the driver was slowly getting out. I do not think she was hurt but she looked upset.

Unit 18

Language

Vocabulary:
gesture, to mean, people, hands, arms, language, different, same, how often, countries, really

Developments

[A] (ii) Picture 3 is Betty Sharp.
    (iii) She's got short hair.
        It's black.
        She rides a bike.
        She comes here every day.
        She's got a long, red scarf.
        She's quite tall.

[B] (i) He works in the office downstairs.
        He always drives a Mini.
        He's good looking.
        He's got glasses.
        He smokes.
        He's very funny.
    (ii) has/have got – 1 example:
            He's got glasses...
        Simple Present – 5 examples:
            like, works, drives, smokes, makes
        to be + adjective – 3 examples:
            I'm glad, he's good-looking, he's very funny

Unit 19

Language

Necessity:
1 a 2 b 3 b 4 a

Developments

[A] to catch the fly; to catch the spider; to catch the fly; to catch the bird; to catch the cat, etc.

Unit 20

Developments

[A] 1 The Brown family are Nicola's in-laws.
    Venisha's uncles:
    Martin, Thomas, Harry, Arnold, Dwayne

    Venisha's aunts:
    Susan, Rita, Angela, Jan

    Venisha's cousins:
    Maurice, Sarah, Francis, Jamila, Asher

    Nicola's nieces:
    Sarah, Jamila, Asher

    Nicola's nephews:
    Maurice, Francis

  2 Wedding in the family:

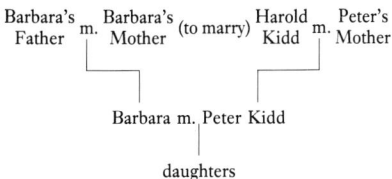

[B] Hippos die – a
    Rogue's return – b
    Life after death – c
    Tip is just the ticket – d
    Sad nose – e
    Couple leave for Russian climb – f
    Burns advance – g

Unit 21

Language

How questions:
1 d 2 c 3 b 4 a

Simple Present in the future:
travel, explore, leave, drive, visit, leave

Developments

[A] Echuca
[B] a High Street
    b Paddle Wheel Motel on left
    c Left at crossroads into Heygarth Street
    d House on right, tree in garden

Unit 22

Language

Future obligation:
... we all have to move
... because I'm going to have to leave
... will we have to live in

Vocabulary:
to attract, to consider, to advertise, to move, to save, to include, to make contact, to set up

Developments

Here are Arthur C. Clarke's answers:
1 a 2 b 3 b 4 a 5 a 6 f 7 c
8 a 9 e 10 b 11 a 12 b 13 b
14 a 15 b

How many of your answers are the same as Clarke's? Count them.

0–2 You are very pessimistic about the future, it worries you. Learn to value the advantages of science and technology.
3–5 You need to prepare yourself better for life in the next century.
6–7 You are interested in the future and you can see some of the changes that are going to come.
8–9 You are enthusiastic and knowledgeable about the future world. Your children will be astronauts and your grandchildren will be spacebabies.

10–13 Book your seat on the Space Shuttle! You already live in a future world.

14–15 Did you look at the scores first? Or are you Arthur C. Clarke? Only 1% get this score.

Unit 23

Developments

[A]

```
                                    (Your address)
(Date)
Winnipeg Advanced Education College,
Hillside Drive,
Winnipeg.
Dear Sir or Madam,
   Please send me details of your courses
in Computer Programming.
   Thanking you in advance.
        Yours faithfully,
```

[B]

```
                                    (Your address)
(Date)
Sea View Hotel,
Harbour Road,
Cork,
Ireland.
Dear Sir or Madam,
   I would like to book a double room with bath
for 2 weeks from the 1st to the 14th of August
inclusive.
   I look forward to receiving your
confirmation.
        Yours faithfully,
```

Unit 24

Developments

[A] rumpus = a disturbance
I = Andrew
It's about someone who went away on a boat.

[B] Sorry Mum! 5, 10, 6, 9, 8, 2, 12
Polecat 7, 3, 14, 1, 13, 4, 11

[C] Verbs of communication:
to tell, to talk, to say, to add, to notify

[D] 1 to be terrified
2 to land
3 aircraft
4 laws
5 *run* (not *ran*)

Grammar Reference

1 Key to phonetic symbols

iː	see	ʊ	good	aɪ	by
ɪ	big	uː	soon	aʊ	how
e	get	ʌ	bus	ɔɪ	boy
æ	man	ɜː	third	ɪə	near
ɑː	bath	ə	away	eə	fair
ɒ	top	eɪ	day	ʊə	sure
ɔː	saw	əʊ	go		

p	pen	f	fine	h	help
b	book	v	very	m	mine
t	time	θ	think	n	new
d	dog	ð	that	ŋ	long
k	can	s	say	l	long
g	game	z	zoo	r	room
tʃ	cheap	ʃ	shop	j	yes
dʒ	job	ʒ	measure	w	water

2 Pronouns

Direct	Indirect	Possessive	Possessive Adjectives
I	me	mine	my
you	you	yours	your
she	her	hers	her
he	him	his	his
it	it	its	its
we	us	ours	our
you	you	yours	your
they	them	theirs	their

3 To be

Present: I am, you are, she/he/it is, we are, you are, they are
Past: I was, you were, she/he/it was, we were, you were, they were

4 Regular Verbs, e.g. to walk

Imperative – walk
Simple Present – walk/walks
Simple Past – walked
Present Participle – walking

5 Common Irregular Verbs

become	became
begin	began
break	broke
build	built
buy	bought
catch	caught
choose	chose
come	came
cost	cost
do	did
drink	drank
drive	drove
eat	ate
fall	fell
feel	felt
fight	fought
find	found
forget	forgot
freeze	froze
get	got
give	gave
go	went
have	had
keep	kept
know	knew
learn	learnt/learned
leave	left
let	let
light	lit/lighted
lose	lost
make	made
mean	meant
meet	met
pay	paid
read	read
ring	rang
run	ran
say	said
sell	sold
send	sent
shoot	shot
shut	shut
sing	sang
sit	sat
sleep	slept
speak	spoke
spell	spelt/spelled
stand	stood
swim	swam
take	took
teach	taught
tell	told
think	thought
understand	understood
wear	wore
win	won
write	wrote

Oxford University Press
Walton Street, Oxford OX2 6DP

Oxford New York Toronto Delhi Bombay
Calcutta Madras Karachi Petaling Jaya
Singapore Hong Kong Tokyo Nairobi
Dar es Salaam Cape Town Melbourne
Auckland

and associated companies in
Beirut Berlin Ibadan Nicosia

OXFORD is a trade mark of
Oxford University Press

ISBN 0 19 433587 9

© Oxford University Press 1988

First published 1988

All rights reserved. No part of this publication may be reproduced, stored in a retrieval system, or transmitted, in any form or by any means, electronic, mechanical, photocopying, recording, or otherwise, without the prior permission of Oxford University Press.

This book is sold subject to the condition that it shall not, by way of trade or otherwise, be lent, re-sold, hired or otherwise circulated without the publisher's prior consent in any form of binding or cover other than that in which it is published and without a similar condition including this condition being imposed on the subsequent purchaser.

Phototypeset by Tradespools Limited, Frome, Somerset

Printed in Hong Kong

Acknowledgements

The authors would like to thank Sylvia Chalker, Paul Martin, Cary Whitworth, Steve Norman, Barbara Webb, Giori Raman, Richard Udall, Viki Thorpe and everyone else who helped with comments, suggestions and advice. They would also like to thank Alan Maley for his comments in the early stages of the project.

Thanks also for help with particular pieces of material to Ursula Nixon and Brian Brownlea.

Our special thanks go to Jane, Angela and Peter Lodge and Elisa for all their help and support, also to Yvonne de Henseler, Avril Price-Budgen, Mike Brain, Jane Davies, Liz Hunter, Carole White, and everyone at OUP who have given so much hard work, encouragement and inspiration to the project.

The publishers and authors would like to thank the following for their kind permission to use articles, extracts or adaptations from copyright material:

The Bangkok Post, British Rail, Penny Chorlton (*Bobbing Up and Down Like This*), *The Daily Mirror*, *The Guardian*, Martyn Lewis (*And Finally*, Century Publications), *The Observer*, *Omni* Magazine (The Arther C Clarke Quiz), The Press Association, Peterborough Development Corporation, Reuters, *Save the Children Magazine*, *The Sun*, *The Sunday Express*, *The Sunday Times*, Trailfinders Ltd., *You* Magazine (King Rat)

Illustrations by:

Paul Allen, David Ashby, Christina Balit, Ann Blockley, Leo Duff, Antonia Enthoven, Martin Faulkner, Gary Hincks, Roy Ingram, Kevin Jones Associates, Robert Kettell, Kim Lane, Sally Lecky-Thompson, Mandy Li, Frances Lloyd, David Murray, Bill Piggins, Bill Prosser, Graham Rawle, RDH Artists, Mark Rowney, Paul Thomas

Studio and location photographs by:

Martyn Chillmaid, Rob Judges, Mark Mason, Terry Williams

The publishers would like to thank the following for their permission to reproduce photographs:

Associated Press, The Aviation Picture Library, BBC Hulton Picture Library, Beken of Cowes, Brenard Photographic Services, Britannia Airways, Bruce Coleman Ltd., Colorado Nature Photographic Studio, Devon News, Jane Duff, Express Newspapers, Paul Felix, Format Photographers, Richard & Sally Greenhill, Guinness World of Records, Robert Harding, Hutchison Library, Image Bank, Impact, Independent Television News Ltd.: Channel 4 News, Frank Lane Agency, The National Gallery, Network, Oxford Scientific Films, P & O Ferries, Photo Source, Press Association, Rex Features, The Royal Archives, J Sainsbury Ltd., Save the Children Fund, Harry Shunk, Syndication International, Stephen Taylor Woodrow, Topham, Tropix, Gerhard Vormwald, Zefa

and the following for their time and assistance:

Currys Ltd., Oxford; Jem-i-Ni (Oxford) Ltd; Morris Photographic Centre, Oxford; Oxford Information Centre; Le Petit Blanc, Oxford; The Prince of Wales, Oxford; Touchwood Sports, Oxford.